The
Wisdom
of
Tea

Noriko Morishita is a Japanese author and reporter. Since publishing her experiences as a writer in *Nori-yakko Dosue*, she has enjoyed a successful career as an essayist and writer of reportage. A film adaptation of *Nichi Nichi Kore Kōjitsu* (the Japanese original text for *The Wisdom of Tea*) was released in 2018.

Eleanor Goldsmith was born in Wales and has worked as a translator since 2000. She now lives in Auckland, New Zealand, where she continues to practise Tea. She is President of the Chado Urasenke Tankokai New Zealand Association.

The Wisdom of Tea

Life Lessons from the Japanese Tea Ceremony

NORIKO MORISHITA

Translated by Eleanor Goldsmith

ALLEN&UNWIN

First published in the United Kingdom by Allen & Unwin in 2020

This paperback edition first published in the United Kingdom by Allen & Unwin in 2021

First Japanese edition published in 2002 by Asuka Shinsha Ltd., Tokyo

Japanese paperback edition published in 2008 by SHINCHOSHA Publishing Co., Ltd., Tokyo.

First English edition published in Japan as *Every Day a Good Day: Fifteen lessons I learned about happiness from Japanese tea culture* by Japan Publishing Industry Foundation for Culture in 2019 as part of the JAPAN LIBRARY project.

This English edition to be distributed in the United Kingdom and Commonwealth (excluding Australia, New Zealand and Canada) and published by arrangement with SHINCHOSHA Publishing Co., Ltd. c/o Tuttle-Mori Agency, Inc.

Nichinichi Kore Kojitsu: Ocha ga oshietekureta 15 no shiawase © Noriko Morishita 2002.

Translated by Eleanor Goldsmith
English translation copyright © Japan Publishing Industry Foundation for Culture, 2019
The moral right of the translator has been asserted.

Photography by Katsuhiko Ushiro
Additional photography by Mitsuyoshi Hirano (Shinchosha Photography Department) where noted by an asterisk [*]

Illustrations (Tea Terms) by Itsu Okamura

The moral right of Noriko Morishita to be identified as the author of this work has been asserted by her in accordance with the Copyright, Designs and Patents Act of 1988.

Every effort has been made to trace or contact all copyright holders. The publishers will be pleased to make good any omissions or rectify any mistakes brought to their attention at the earliest opportunity.

JAPAN LIBRARY

Allen & Unwin
c/o Atlantic Books
Ormond House
26–27 Boswell Street
London WC1N 3JZ

www.allenandunwin.com/uk

A CIP catalogue record for this book is available from the British Library.

Paperback ISBN 978 1 91163 064 7
E-Book ISBN 978 1 76087 304 2

Printed and bound in Great Britain by TJ Books Limited, Padstow, Cornwall

FSC
MIX
Paper | Supporting
responsible forestry
FSC® C013056
www.fsc.org

10 9 8 7 6 5

Product safety EU representative: Authorised Rep Compliance Ltd., Ground Floor, 71 Lower Baggot Street, Dublin, D02 P593, Ireland. www.arccompliance.com

Translator's Note: The Hepburn system of romanization is used for Japanese terms, including the names of persons and places. Long vowels in Japanese words are represented by macrons, except in familiar place names. Japanese names are given in Western order—personal name first, surname last—with the exception of certain historical figures like Sen no Rikyū, who are better known by their names in Japanese order. Practitioners of the Way of Tea avoid the term "tea ceremony," so this cultural practice is generally rendered in the text as "Tea," much as the Chinese philosophical tradition Dao is often translated simply as "the Way." Romanized Tea terminology is used liberally in the text as a means of enabling the reader to accompany the author on her journey along this initially baffling path, but a list of tea terms is provided at the end for reference.

CONTENTS

FOREWORD

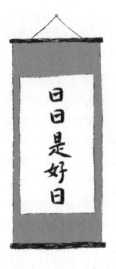

Foreword

Every Saturday afternoon, I walk to a house about ten minutes away from my own. It is an old house, with a big paperplant in a pot outside the entrance. Rattling open the sliding door, I am greeted by glistening water droplets on the entrance hall floor and the smooth scent of charcoal. From the garden, I hear a faint babble of running water.

I enter a quiet room overlooking that garden to kneel on the tatami-covered floor, boil water, whisk tea, and drink it. And I simply repeat that process—again and again.

I have been coming to this weekly Tea lesson for twenty-five years, since I was a university student.

Even now, I often get the procedures wrong. Many elements remain opaque to me, making me wonder why we do them at all. My feet go numb. The etiquette frustrates me. I have no idea how long it will take me to understand everything completely. "What's so great about Tea, anyway?" friends sometimes ask me. "Why have you carried on with it for so long?"

When I was ten years old, my parents took me to see a film called *La Strada,* directed by Federico Fellini. One can only describe this tale of poor itinerant entertainers as bleak. Its meaning escaped me entirely, and I could not understand why a movie like this was considered a masterpiece. To my mind, it had nothing on Disney.

But when I watched it again ten years later, as a university student, I was shocked. Gelsomina's theme song sounded familiar to me, but apart from that it was like seeing the film for the first time.

So that was what La Strada *was all about,* I thought. I sat in the pitch-black movie theater crying my eyes out, my heartstrings torn to shreds.

In the years that followed, I fell in love and experienced the trauma of heartbreak myself. Suffering setback after setback in my search for a job, I continued to seek my own place in the world. After a decade and more of these admittedly pedestrian struggles, I watched *La Strada* again in my mid-thirties.

Once more, there were so many scenes that I did not remember seeing before, lines that I did not recall having heard. Giulietta Masina's flawless performance as the naive heroine Gelsomina was painfully poignant. Zampanò, too, was no longer simply a cruel brute; lying prostrate on the beach under the stars, his body wracked with sobs, he now seemed a pitiful old man as he mourned the death of the girl he had abandoned. *Humans are such miserable creatures,* I thought. Tears rolled down my face in an endless stream.

Each time I watched *La Strada*, it was an entirely different film. And it deepened with every viewing.

In this world, there are things that we understand immediately and things that take time to comprehend. Once is enough for the former type of experience. But things in the latter category, like Fellini's *La Strada,* reveal themselves to us only gradually, undergoing a slow metamorphosis over multiple encounters. And each time we understand a little more, we realize that we had only been seeing a tiny fragment of the whole.

Tea is exactly like that.

When I was twenty, I thought of Tea as nothing but etiquette and rules. There was nothing pleasant about that feeling of being forced into a mold. What made the situation worse was that I had no idea what I was doing, no matter how many times I did it. And even though I could not remember a single thing, the procedures and combinations of utensils would change according to the weather or climatic conditions that very day. When the seasons changed, the layout of the whole room would be drastically altered. I experienced the endless cycles of the tea room for years and years with only the vaguest awareness of what it all meant.

Then one day, quite out of the blue, I noticed the tepid smell of rain in the air. *Oh, there's a shower on the way,* I thought. The droplets that pelted the trees and plants in the garden sounded different from before. Afterward, the air was musty with the smell of earth.

Until that moment, I had only ever thought of rain as water—and odorless water, at that—that fell from the sky. Soil had not had a smell, either. It was as though I had been looking out at the world from within an upturned glass jar, and then someone had lifted the glass and let the seasons reach my senses of smell and hearing. It reminded me that I too was a seasonal creature, no different from a frog that could identify the smell of the pond where it was born.

*

The cherry blossom always reached full bloom in early April each year. In mid-June, the rain would start to pour down, as if by appointment. I was astounded by this entirely unremarkable fact, which had taken me almost until the age of thirty to notice.

Before that point, I had thought of the seasons in binary terms: hot seasons and cold ones. Little by little, finer categories began to emerge. In spring, flowering quince bloomed first, followed by plum, peach, and then cherry trees. Once the last of these had turned from pink to freshest green, the heady scent of blossom-laden wisteria tendrils would waft through the neighborhood. After the azaleas had passed their peak, the air would become muggy, heralding the first showers of the rainy season. Plums would swell on the trees, irises would line the streams and ponds, hydrangeas would burst into flower, and the sweet fragrance of gardenias would drift by. When the hydrangeas faded and the rainy season had come to an end, succulent cherries and peaches would fill the greengrocer's shelves. Each season overlapped with the next, so there was always something to enjoy.

The traditional Japanese calendar was divided into not four, but twenty-four seasons. To me, though, it actually seemed like a different season every time I went to my weekly Tea lesson.

One day, when it was pouring down, I became so absorbed in the sound of the rain that the room seemed to disappear, leaving me right in the middle of the deluge. As I listened, I eventually *became* the rain falling on the plants in Sensei's garden.

So this is what it means to be alive!
My skin was prickly with goosebumps.

Moments like this have come to me from time to time over my years studying Tea, like fixed-term deposits reaching maturity. I did not do anything special to spark them. I lived the life of a perfectly ordinary twentysomething and continued through my thirties and forties in a similarly unremarkable vein.

Without my noticing it, though, something had been building all that time, like water filling a cup drop by drop. Nothing would change until the cup was full. The water eventually reached the top and bulged above the rim, held in place only by surface tension until, one day, another drop fell and broke the equilibrium. In that instant, the water spilled over the edge and flowed out.

We do not have to study Tea to experience a gradual awakening, of course. Men who have become fathers often say things like, "My old man used to tell me that I'd understand one day, but it was only when I held my own child in my arms that I realized what he meant." Some people find that, when they get sick, entirely commonplace things in their surroundings become incredibly dear to them.

The passage of time alone can open our eyes on occasion to how much we have grown. But there is nothing like Tea for paring away the excess and providing a tangible sense of the personal growth that you cannot see. You haven't the faintest clue what you are doing at first. Then, one day, out of the blue, your horizons broaden. Just like in life.

In exchange for the time it takes to understand, Tea lets you savor the thrill of that moment when your world expands, as first a small cup, then a bigger one, and eventually an enormous pot of water overflows, again and again.

Just after I turned forty, when I had been studying Tea for more than twenty years, I began to talk to my friends about it. They would react with amazement, saying things like, "Wow! Is that really what it's like?" This reaction surprised me in turn. Many people imagine Tea to be an expensive pastime for highbrow sophisticates, but they have no idea what feelings the practice of Tea inspires. I had completely forgotten this, even though I had been among those people until not long before.

That was when I decided to write about Tea one day. About what I had felt during my lessons at Sensei's house, about the multitude of seasons, about those moments over the last twenty-five years when my cup had overflowed.

Beyond my comprehension as a child, Fellini's *La Strada* makes the person I am today weep buckets. It breaks my heart effortlessly; I don't need to strain to understand it. There are some things that cannot be understood until the time is right, no matter how you try. But when the day of understanding comes, there is no disguising it.

When I began to learn Tea, I could not hold on to the tiniest inkling of what I was doing, no matter how hard I tried. But, step by step, things have started to come into focus. After twenty-five years, I now have at least a hazy grasp of why we do what we do.

When you are living through difficult times, when you have lost all confidence and the world seems plunged into darkness, Tea teaches you one thing above all else: live in the moment with an eye to the future.

INTRODUCTION

Chajin:
A Person of Tea

Aunt Takeda

"She's quite something, you know," my mother said. I was fourteen, and she had just returned from a parents' association meeting at my younger brother's school. "We all bowed to each other, but her bow was different from the rest."

"What do you mean, her bow was different?" I asked.

"It was just an ordinary bow, but *different* somehow," Mom replied. "When she said, 'My name is Takeda,' and lowered her head, it took my breath away. I've never seen such a beautiful bow."

"And her name is Mrs. Takeda?"

"Yes. She's really quite something."

What kind of person is "quite something," I wonder?

For some reason I imagined someone severe and intimidating.

One day, I found my mother standing on our doorstep chatting with a middle-aged woman in a round collar blouse whom I had never seen before. With her fair complexion and soft, gentle demeanor, she somehow reminded me of a *habutae-mochi* rice cake.

"Oh, is this your daughter?" she asked. "Pleased to meet you. My name is Takeda." And then, with a warm smile that lit up her eyes, she bowed.

So this was the woman my mother had mentioned. She certainly had a nice, smooth bow, but I did not think it was as special as my mother had made out. She was a world away from the kind of person I had imagined when I heard the words "quite something."

She's just a nice, friendly middle-aged lady.

And that was how I met Tomoko Takeda.

Mrs. Takeda became close enough friends with my mother for me to address her as Aunt Takeda. She was a native of one of Yokohama's working-class districts. Born in 1932, she had—unusually for a woman of her generation—pursued a career into her thirties. Then she had married, had children, and settled into the life of a full-time housewife.

Aunt Takeda had a kind of well-groomed air about her. It was not that she was a great beauty, and I never saw her wear even a single piece of jewelry, but she always looked lovely, nonetheless.

She never smiled in that ambiguous way middle-aged women often do, as though concealing something, nor did she ever speak in the shrill, strident voice so common among such ladies when they flock together. Her brisk manner of speaking, which marked her out as a true-born Yokohama-ite, was quite at odds with her soft, gentle demeanor.

While she was always perfectly proper in her dealings with others, she appeared to dislike crowds, so once the task at hand was completed she would swiftly excuse herself from the group and leave on her own. Unlike the many grown-ups—men and women alike—I knew who spoke or acted differently in the presence of authority or power, Aunt Takeda did not change for anyone.

When I failed to get into my first-choice university and was wondering whether to spend another year studying to retake the entrance examination, my parents and the other adults I knew all said exactly the same thing: "You're a girl, so there's no need for you to take a year off. You'll get married and stop working someday, after all. Just go to another university."

Only Aunt Takeda thought differently. "Go where you want to go, Noriko," she told me. "I think women should have a career and live life to the fullest."

It was the first time I had heard a middle-aged woman clearly voice her own opinion. And when I eventually decided not to try the exam again, she said, "I see. As long as you've made up your own mind, that's fine. Now you must live your life in a way that makes you glad you reached the conclusion that you did."

Aunt Takeda always conjured up an aura of composure and richness, but not in the same way as the wives of the wealthy. In a time when the vast majority of housewives spent their lives focused only on their husband's career advancement and their children's academic success, she seemed familiar with a broader adult world.

"It's because she's a *chajin*," Mom explained.

"What's a *chajin*?" I asked.

"A 'person of Tea'—someone who does tea ceremony. She's been studying it since she was a girl, I hear. Apparently she's even got a license to teach. There's definitely something different about her. I spotted it immediately, the very first time I saw her. She's quite something."

I made a noncommittal noise in reply.

Tea was like something from another planet to me. All I knew was that you went *swish-swish* to froth up the foam and then turned the tea bowl before drinking for some reason. I had no idea what studying Tea had to do with Aunt Takeda's indescribably well-groomed air or her unflappable nature. But the dignified sound of the word *chajin* when I heard it that first time stuck with me.

My student years passed in the blink of an eye.

I had wanted to use my time at university to find something I could devote my life to, but I did not know what I really wanted to do. I kept searching for the unusual, attracted to things that few others were interested in, but failed to stick with any of them for long. In my third year of university, people around me were beginning to bring up the subject of finding a job.

One day, Mom suddenly turned to me and said, "Noriko, why don't you learn Tea?"

"Huh? Why should I?" I asked, frowning reflexively. I had not given even a nanosecond's thought to the idea before.

For one thing, hobbies like flower arranging and Tea were outdated and desperately uncool. In my mind, they were all lumped together as pursuits that conservative parents who regarded marriage as a form of job-hunting forced on their daughters to ensure that they married money. If I was going to take up a hobby, I would prefer flamenco or Italian.

No, Tea was a world that required oodles of money. It was a status symbol for the wealthy. Nothing but meaningless authoritarianism. Just women showing off to each other. Nothing about it appealed to me in the slightest. However . . .

"Tea? Oh, that sounds great. I'd love to learn it!" piped up a voice. It was my cousin Michiko, her eyes alight.

Michiko and I were the same age and had been fast friends ever since we were little. Her family were well-off and lived far away in one of Japan's provincial regions. Whenever the summer or winter vacation rolled around, I would go and stay with them, and the two of us would spend weeks together. She had moved to the big city for university and was living in an apartment nearby.

Now she said, "I've been wanting to learn Tea for a while." She was a sweet-natured young woman and much more cooperative than me.

"Well, then, by all means, go ahead," my mother replied. "It'll be good for you." Then she leaned forward and said to me, "See? Michiko's going to give it a try, like a good girl."

I felt a pang of resentment. But when Michiko said to me, "Come on, Nori, let's go together. Let's study Tea!" I wavered despite my irritation.

If I went to Tea lessons with Michiko, we could stop off at a coffee shop for a chat on our way home. Whenever we got together, we would gab for hours about the latest movies that we had seen, our favorite foreign stars, interesting novels, and traveling overseas.

I only had one more year of university life left and I still had not found anything I really wanted to do. If I was honest with myself, I was sick to the back teeth of chasing the unusual wherever I could find it. Perhaps it would be better to start something—anything—in earnest, rather than staying frustrated about not finding what I wanted.

And I really did mean anything. Even one of those stuffy old Japanese traditions . . .

"I'll ask Mrs. Takeda," said Mom. "Even you'd be happy with her as your teacher, right?"

When I heard Mom say that, images of Aunt Takeda's inexpressible composure and neatness came to me as the echoes from that word *chajin* began to resonate again deep in my heart.

"Well, I suppose I could give it a try . . ."

It was the spring of 1977, and I was twenty years old.

CHAPTER 1

Learn That You Know Nothing

Sensei's House

Aunt Takeda taught tea to several neighborhood housewives at her home on Wednesday afternoons, but as Michiko and I were university students and had classes on weekdays, she agreed to teach the two of us on Saturdays instead.

I had passed her house many times. It stood beside the railway tracks about ten minutes' walk from my own home, an old two-story wooden house with a tile roof and a soba noodle shop next door. A big paperplant sat outside the entrance in a pot.

We had been unsure what to wear and if we needed to bring anything.

"Oh, ordinary clothes are fine. Just come along this Saturday, anyway," she had said.

It was just after the string of public holidays in early May. Feeling slightly nervous, we passed through the gate to Aunt Takeda's house, me wearing a blouse and skirt, and Michiko—about to meet Aunt Takeda for the first time—wearing a suit.

We rattled open the sliding door to find an entrance hall as spotless as a traditional inn's. The floor glistened with water droplets and not even a single pair of shoes had been left lying around, unlike at my house.

"Hello?"

My call elicited an answering "Coming!" from somewhere deep within the house, followed by the sound of bustling footsteps. The dyed noren curtain flipped open to reveal that familiar round, fair-skinned face.

For a moment I was lost for words. I had never seen Aunt Takeda wearing kimono before. It was a soft shade of beige that suited her pale complexion perfectly and gave her a neat, smart look.

"Welcome," she said. "Do please come in."

This was the first time that I had been inside Aunt Takeda's house. The wooden pillars and hallway were the rich golden-brown of hard-baked rice crackers. Stepping up from the entrance hall, we were shown to the innermost of two adjoining formal rooms, its floor covered in eight of the traditional woven rush mats called tatami.

"Just wait here a minute," Aunt Takeda told us.

It was an astonishingly empty space. Michiko and I slowly gazed around us. This was where we would have our weekly Tea lesson from now on. Looking up at the high ceiling, we saw the elaborate latticework of the transom between this room and the next. Hanging in the large *tokonoma* alcove set into one wall was a long scroll. There was also a framed piece of calligraphy on a picture rail.

Across the hallway, through the glass door, we could see a garden. It was not large, but stone lanterns and small boulders were dotted around here and there, and the persimmon and plum trees were lush with verdant new leaves. Blossom-laden wisteria tendrils swayed in the breeze. The dense azalea bushes were still a riot of red and pink flowers, making them look like origami pomanders.

A white surfboard that must have belonged to Aunt Takeda's son was propped up beyond the persimmon tree in the garden, while her daughter's piano stood against the wall of the hallway.

But the room we had been shown into had not even a whiff of everyday household clutter. It was clean and somehow filled with an air of tension, but had, nonetheless, a warmth that must have come from years of use. It reminded me of Aunt Takeda herself: not glamorous, but well-groomed; friendly, yet somehow firm.

Michiko and I kneeled in the formal posture, to which we were unaccustomed.

"Nori?" Michiko whispered.

"What?" For some reason, I lowered my voice, too.

"What does that say?"

Michiko was looking at the flowing calligraphy on the scroll in the alcove and in the frame above the picture rail opposite.

". . . I can't read it."

Entering the room, Aunt Takeda followed the direction of our gaze and smiled broadly.

"The one in the frame says, 'Every day is a good day,'" she told us. "And today's scroll says, 'The bamboo leaves make a refreshing breeze.' It's the season of new leaves, so it's perfect for you youngsters, don't you think?"

Folding the *Fukusa*

I had imagined that a tea lesson would start with a talk about the rules of tea or something like that. But the first thing that Aunt Takeda did was hand each of us a thin cardboard box, about a centimetre deep. Opening the lid, I found that it contained a square of cloth in a vivid shade similar to the vermilion ink pad used to stamp documents with a personal seal.

"This is called a *fukusa*," she told us.

About the size of a man's handkerchief, it was made of silk, folded over and sewn together on three sides. The thick fabric was soft but heavy in my hand.

Saying "We start by wearing this at the waist," Aunt Takeda lightly grasped a corner of the cloth and folded it into a triangle before tucking the tip into her obi. Still mystified, Michiko and I each tucked our own *fukusa* into the belt of our skirt. The triangle of vermilion cloth hung at my left hip.

"Watch," she said. With her left hand, Aunt Takeda swiftly pulled the *fukusa* from her obi, took hold of one corner with her right, then slid the left down to grasp the other and form an inverted triangle. Then she let the silk fabric sag slightly before vigorously pulling it taut again.

Snap! went the cloth.

We tried tugging on both ends of our *fukusa*, too. A rhythmical *snap! snap!* rang out.

"This is called *chiriuchi*—casting off dust," she explained.

Next, Aunt Takeda shifted her fingertips and, in a fluid motion, folded the *fukusa* vertically into thirds, like a folding screen. Then she folded it in half along its length and in half again, making a small square of cloth that fit into the palm of her hand. Her fingers moved smoothly, like creatures in their own right. We watched and copied what she did.

"This is *fukusa-sabaki*—folding the *fukusa*," she told us.

"I see . . ." I replied.

Natsume and Matcha

Aunt Takeda slipped behind a sliding paper screen and returned carrying something round and black in the palm of her hand. Shaped like a flat-topped egg and glossy as a watermelon seed, the little lacquerware container looked something like the lidded dishes used for steamed egg custard.

"This is a *natsume*. It's the container that holds the tea," she explained.

The *natsume* was acorn-smooth, with a lid that fit snugly onto its body. Picking it up, I found it to be surprisingly light. I lifted off the lid—which seemed strangely reluctant to part from the body and let air inside—to reveal a mound of grass-green powder within. It was a vibrant, almost synthetic shade.

That's tea?!

This was the first time I had seen *matcha* in its powdered form. When I replaced the lid, I again felt a sensation of resistance, with an almost imperceptible hiss of air.

"You use your *fukusa* to wipe the *natsume*," Aunt Takeda told us. Then, grasping the folded *fukusa* in her right hand and picking up the *natsume* with her left, she said, "Wipe the far side, then the near one, following the curve of the lid. Just like writing the hiragana character *ko*."

Using the rounded fold of the *fukusa,* she gently drew the character on the *natsume*'s lid.

Why ko, *with its gap in the middle?* I wondered. *Surely it would be better to wipe the whole surface?* But I wiped the lid just as she had said to.

The First Bowl of Tea

"Right, then. Since today's your first day, I'll make tea for you."

Aunt Takeda brought us a tray on which she had placed two small plates, each of which bore a small, white *manjū* bun. A purple flower design was faintly visible through the bun's thin outer layer.

"This is called an iris *manjū.* We serve them only in May, to mark the seasonal festival," she explained.

"I see."

I was a die-hard fan of Western confectionery, like pies and cream puffs and chocolate cake, and had only ever thought of Japanese sweets as something elderly people liked.

"Go ahead and eat it," Aunt Takeda said.

I was baffled. Where was the tea? I was worried that the *manjū* bun might stick in my throat without something to wash it down.

7

Michiko was eyeing her *manjū* wordlessly beside me as well. "Go on, eat it up."

At her urging, we each picked up our bun and stuffed it into our mouth. Aunt Takeda started the tea-making process. I had never seen it done at such close quarters.

She glided in and out with utensils, opened lids, poured hot water, and raised something that looked like a bamboo whisk several times as though inspecting it. Her movements were flowing, almost like a dance. At one stage, she seemed to be wiping the tea bowl with a white cloth.

I had no idea what was going on, but it did not appear to be all that difficult.

She put some of the bright green powder into the tea bowl, poured in some hot water and began to whisk: *Swish-swish-swish-swish . . .*

Yes, that's it! That's Tea!

Slurping When You Drink

Finally the tea was placed before us.

When I visited Ryōanji Temple as a young teenager during a trip to Kyoto with my family, we had each been served a black tea bowl containing a tiny amount of liquid covered in a dense green foam. My parents drank it with every appearance of enjoyment, but my younger brother and I screwed up our faces at the bitterness when we took a sip.

Why do adults enjoy drinking such bitter things?

Thinking back, all grownup drinks tasted bitter when I tried them. It was the same when I had my first sip of coffee, and when I tried beer, too.

I had not had *matcha* since then.

In the bottom of the tea bowl, the kale-juice-colored puddle of *matcha* was half-covered with froth.

"You should drink your *matcha* in about two and a half sips," Aunt Takeda explained. "At the end, you make a slight slurping sound, to make sure none is left."

"Really? We have to slurp it?"

"That's right. At the end. It's also a sign that you've finished drinking."

As a child, I used to make a gurgling noise when drinking juice through a straw. But, after repeated scoldings about how eating soup noisily was considered the height of vulgarity in the West, these days I could not help but blush if I heard one of my uncles from a rural backwater slurping his way through his potage at a hotel wedding reception.

Ugh . . .

Still somewhat reluctant, I took two sips and then, mustering my courage, put my heart and soul into the third. *Slurp!* For an instant, I felt a blood-curdling chill concentrated in the region of my ears, but the embarrassment turned out to be merely momentary once I had tried it. In fact, the feeling was actually quite delightful. The reluctance that I had felt a minute before vanished in a flash.

9

As expected, the tea was bitter. However, the bitterness had washed away the sweet aftertaste of the *manjū*, as if it had been carried away by the tide.

On our way home that day, Michiko and I laughed about our little taste of culture shock.

"Isn't it funny how you have to snap the *fukusa*?"

"Slurping when you drink is weird, too, don't you think?"

We would encounter even more mystifying things at our second tea lesson.

"It doesn't matter why"

At our second lesson, we got to touch that swishy whisk used to stir the tea.

"This is called a *chasen*," Aunt Takeda told us. The fine bamboo prongs curled inward at their tips. Aunt Takeda placed the *chasen* into a tea bowl containing a small amount of hot water and repeated a strange series of gestures three times, describing an arc with the whisk and slowly raising it almost to the tip of her nose.

"Now you try it."

We too described arcs, each lifting our *chasen* from our bowl. It was an odd feeling, somewhat reminiscent of offering incense at a funeral.

"What are we doing?" I asked.

"What? Oh, you're checking that none of the prongs are broken," Aunt Takeda replied.

"But why do we rotate it like this?"

"It doesn't matter why. This is just what we do."

I didn't understand, but held my tongue.

Aunt Takeda brought out a white linen cloth. "This is a *chakin*," she said. "Watch."

She turned the bowl once, twice, three times, so that the neatly folded *chakin* wiped the rim. After going full circle, she put the little cloth into the bowl and made some fiddly movements with it.

"Finally, you draw the hiragana character *yu*: down the left, up and round to the right, then top to bottom in the middle."

"Why?"

"It doesn't matter why. It doesn't help me if you keep asking 'why?' all the time, either. All you need to know is that we do it like this. You don't need to understand the significance."

It was a curious feeling. At school, my teachers always said, "That was a good question. If you don't understand something, you mustn't accept it without questioning it. Always ask if you don't understand; ask as many times as it takes until you do." So I had always thought that asking the question "why?" was a good thing.

Here, though, it was somehow impolite.

"The reason doesn't matter. We just do it like this. You two might find it hard to accept, but that's just the way it works in Tea."

Hearing such words from the mouth of Aunt Takeda, of all people, was startling.

But at times like that, Aunt Takeda always looked like she was gazing at something dear and much-missed.

"That's just the way it is in Tea. You don't need to know the reason—for now."

O-temae and Walking on Tatami

It was our third tea lesson. The day had finally come to learn how to make tea ourselves.

"The procedure for making tea is called *o-temae*," Aunt Takeda told us. "The most basic form is the thin tea procedure."

We were in a small scullery-like room at the end of the hallway.

"This is the *mizuya*. It's a sort of kitchen for the tea room."

There was a tap, a sink, and a washbowl, with tea bowls and other utensils neatly lined up on the shelves.

Aunt Takeda took a ceramic jar decorated with crisp blue vertical stripes, filled it with fresh cold water, wiped off the stray droplets with a snow-white cloth, and put a black lacquer lid on it.

"First, take this *mizusashi* and sit at the entrance to the tea room."

"*Hai*," I said, acknowledging her instruction.

Aunt Takeda disappeared behind the sliding paper screen into the tea room, the hem of her kimono rustling in her wake.

I carried the heavy *mizusashi* slowly and carefully to the doorway and kneeled down.

"Pick up the *mizusashi* and come in. It's heavy, but hold it level so that the water doesn't slosh around."

To steady the weighty object, I stuck out my elbows and got a firm grip on it, spreading my fingers wide.

"Ah, don't stick your elbows out. Keep your fingers together. Hold it so that the pads of your little fingers just touch the tatami when you put the *mizusashi* down."

"*Hai, hai.*"

"Once is enough."

"*Hai.*"

I tucked my elbows further in and brought my fingers together, making sure that my little fingers were touching the floor. Then, suppressing a grunt of effort, I tensed my body and began to stand. However . . .

"In Tea, we say, 'Handle heavy things lightly and light things as though heavy.'"

Huh? How on earth do you "handle heavy things lightly"?!

In any case, doing my best not to let the effort show in my face, I stood up. I was about to step inside the room when Aunt Takeda spoke again.

"Wait. Always enter the tea room with the left foot. And never tread on the threshold or the borders of the tatami mats. Now, walk as far as the kettle."

You're kidding! There's even a rule about which foot you enter with?

With my left foot, I took a big stride across the threshold. However . . .

"You should cross each tatami mat in exactly six steps. The seventh step takes you onto the next."

At this rate, I won't fit enough steps in!

Shortening my stride to squeeze in the remainder of my six steps, I tiptoed across the mat.

Michiko sat beside Aunt Takeda, unable to utter a sound, her shoulders shaking and her face beet red. Wiping tears from her eyes, she giggled. "You look like some kind of burglar!"

I felt myself blush crimson at the shame of having to be taught how to walk like a toddler at the age of twenty and being treated like a complete incompetent.

Form and Spirit

I had heard rumors that Tea etiquette could be rather finicky. However, the meticulous attention to tiny details was far beyond anything I had imagined.

For example, the simple act of using the *hishaku*—the bamboo ladle—to take a scoop of hot water from the cast iron kettle and pour it into the tea bowl provoked a stream of corrections.

"Ah—you scooped the hot water from the surface just now, didn't you? Hot water should be scooped from the depths of the kettle. In Tea, we say, 'Cold, middle; hot, deep': scoop cold water from the middle of the *mizusashi* and hot water from the very bottom of the kettle."

Surely it doesn't matter if it comes from the top or bottom? It's all from the same kettle. Despite my mental protests, I did as I was told, plunging the ladle deep into the kettle with an audible plop. However . . .

14

"It should be silent—don't let the ladle go plop."

"*Hai.*"

When I went to pour the ladleful of hot water into the tea bowl . . .

"Ah—pour from the front of the bowl, not from the side."

Obediently, I poured from the front of the bowl. The empty ladle dripped, and I tapped it to knock the last few drops off quickly.

"Ah—you mustn't do that. Just hold it still until all the drops have fallen."

Do this, don't do that . . . being picked on about each little thing was starting to get on my nerves. I was bound hand and foot by rules. I did not have a single opportunity to move freely.

Was Aunt Takeda doing this out of spite? I felt like a magician's assistant, curled up tight in a little box with swords being thrust in from every direction.

"In Tea, form comes first. You shape the form first to provide a vessel for the spirit, which comes later."

But creating an empty form without spirit is nothing but formalism! Isn't that just forcing people into a mold? Surely there isn't even a fragment of creativity in simply going through the motions from start to finish, without understanding the meaning?

Feeling squeezed into the mold of Japan's bad old traditions, I was ready to explode with indignation.

Swish-swish

It was something of a relief when the time finally came for me to whisk the tea with the *chasen*.

I'll at least have some freedom when whisking the tea, right?

I furiously swished the bamboo whisk back and forth in short strokes.

"Ah—don't make too many bubbles."

"What?"

This was unexpected. After all, surely *matcha* is meant to have a creamy foam, like a cappuccino?

"Some schools of Tea make it with a dense foam of fine bubbles, but we don't froth it very much in ours. We say you should stir it so that the bubbles die down to reveal the surface of the tea in the shape of a crescent moon."

"A crescent moon?"

How in the world was I meant to leave a "crescent moon" on the foam-covered surface using this wide-ended whisk? It sounded like something a famous swordsman might do in an old adventure novel as a feat of skill.

The Act of Learning

The procedure that Aunt Takeda had completed in no more than fifteen minutes had taken me over an hour. In fact, it felt like twice that to me.

I sat on the floor of the *mizuya*, legs stretched out, flexing my utterly numb toes. As I squirmed at the sharp tingling that accompanied the return of sensation to my feet, I heard Aunt Takeda say, "This is all about practice, too. Soon you'll be able to kneel for hours, quite happily."

Hours? Unbelievable!

She spoke again: "Noriko, why don't you run through that whole procedure again, to see how much you remember? How about it?"

I was lost for words.

I still had pins and needles in my feet, but the words "to see how much you remember" aroused my fierce competitive streak. My academic grades were reasonable. I was supposed to have a fairly good memory. Although my reflexes were a bit slow, people often told me that I was dexterous.

Tea's just a fusty old hobby for housewives, isn't it? It's a piece of cake. I'm going to show Aunt Takeda that I can do it and she'll be so impressed that she'll admit that I have an aptitude for it!

That was certainly part of what drove me to say, "Yes, I'll have another go."

However . . .

I could not walk correctly. I did not know where to sit. I did not know which hand to use, what to pick up, how to pick it up . . . Neither my hands nor my feet would cooperate.

Not one thing I did was right. Nothing had stuck with me, even though I had done it all just an hour before. Each movement seemed to mock me, as if to say, "See? You can't do this, you can't even do that . . ." All I did was respond to commands from start to finish, just like a marionette.

17

And I had looked down on it as a "fusty old hobby for house-wives"! So much for having an aptitude . . .

What should have been a piece of cake was actually well beyond me. Neither my grades at school nor any of the knowledge or common sense that I had learned to date were any help to me here.

"There's no way anyone could remember it all the first time."

The dignified, kimono-clad figure of Aunt Takeda, smiling as she consoled me, somehow seemed unreachably far ahead of me.

I wonder whether the day will come when my *o-temae* flows like hers?

From that moment on, Aunt Takeda became Takeda-sensei, my esteemed teacher.

And one of the scales fell from my eyes.

You mustn't look down on things. You have to start from zero when you learn . . .

Learning means opening yourself up to someone else, accepting that you know nothing. With my scornful assumption that it would be easy for me, I had hobbled my own efforts. How conceited I had been.

Worthless pride is just unnecessary baggage. You have to cast it aside and empty yourself. Otherwise, there is no room to take anything in. *I'll have to start again with a fresh attitude.*

With all my heart, I felt it: "I know nothing . . ."

CHAPTER 2

Don't Think
with Your Head

"Practice Makes Perfect"

We began to practice going through the whole *o-temae*, again and again.

"Bow . . . and take a breath. First, move the *kensui* forward, so that it's in line with your knees."

"*Kensui*?" I echoed, looking around helplessly. The name did not seem to fit any of the utensils.

"It's on your left."

The *kensui* turned out to be the waste water bowl.

"Place the tea bowl in front of you. Now place the *natsume* between the tea bowl and your knees."

I quickly grasped the *natsume* from the side.

"Ah—not like that. This is how you hold the *natsume*." Takeda-sensei placed her hand ever so gently at an angle on the *natsume*'s shoulder and said, "Your hand covers half of the lid, so this is called covering the half-moon . . . Right. And then *fukusa-sabaki*."

I cast the dust off the *fukusa* with a *snap!* and then folded it as she'd taught me.

"Now wipe the lid of the *natsume* as if writing *ko*."

On Sensei's orders, I moved utensils from right to left, wiped with my *fukusa*, opened and closed lids . . . I was simply responding to commands, completely clueless as to what I was doing.

It was no different the third time, nor the fifth, nor even the tenth. I heard exactly the same words each lesson as I moved utensils from right to left, wiped with my *fukusa,* and opened and closed lids.

"Ah—you're holding the *natsume* wrong again. Cover the half-moon."

and

"Don't forget, you pick that up with your right hand and transfer it to your left."

Every lesson, Sensei pointed out dozens of things I was doing wrong.

After our lesson, Michiko and I would stop at a coffee shop on our way home and vent our frustration.

"I don't have a clue what I'm doing!"

"Me neither. Every lesson feels like my first. I can't remember the procedure at all."

"Right? No matter how many times I repeat it, it's exactly the same as when we started."

Each week, Takeda-sensei repeated the same words: "It's all about practice. You've got to do the same thing over and over, as many times as possible. They do say practice makes perfect, after all."

"Right, bow just there. Take a breath. Now move the *kensui* forward. Then the tea bowl. Next the *natsume* . . . That's right. And then *fukusa-sabaki.*"

I repeated the process fifteen times, twenty. I no longer looked around blankly when I heard the words *kensui, chasen,* and *chashaku* (bamboo tea scoop), but I still had no idea what I was doing. I would fold the *fukusa* and then freeze.

"Now, what are you going to do with that *fukusa*?"

Good question.

"Wipe the *natsume*."

Or I would pick up the bamboo ladle only to grind to a halt again.

"What are you doing with that *hishaku* in your hand?"

No idea.

"You can't take a scoop of hot water unless you take the lid off the kettle, can you?"

I could not make a single move without Sensei telling me what to do. It seemed like every lesson would be exactly the same as the first forever if things carried on this way. I tried memorizing the steps in order, counting them off on my fingers.

"Ummm . . . *Kensui*, then tea bowl, then *natsume*, and then . . . ummm . . . *fukusa* . . ."

But Sensei stopped me. "No!" she said sharply. "You mustn't memorize it! It's no good trying to remember it with your head. Practice is about going through it as many times as you can, until your hands start to move of their own accord."

What on earth was she talking about? It was absurd to correct me about all those little things and then tell me not to remember them. How else could I learn such complicated, finicky movements?

Different Utensils Every Week

Takeda-sensei did another thing that exasperated us. Each time we arrived for our lesson, a new utensil that we had never seen before was waiting for us in the *mizuya*.

"When you wipe this tea container, you don't draw the character *ko*. Write the kanji *ni* instead—two parallel horizontal lines."

or

"The lid of this *mizusashi* is split in two, right down the middle."

There was always something to remember about the procedure for using these new utensils, and always something to be corrected on. *Tana*—portable shelf units for displaying utensils—began to make an appearance. Round *tana*, square *tana*, *tana* with a drawer . . . Each type needed to be handled in a different way.

Even though we had not yet grasped the basic procedure, we had to tailor our *o-temae* to different equipment each time. Whenever we saw a new utensil, a sigh would escape our lips: *Again?!* There was no way anyone could remember it all. One day, I tried to make a note of something, but the moment I did, Takeda-sensei's voice rang out: "No! You mustn't take notes during your lesson."

I was bewildered. Why was she scolding me, instead of praising me for my diligence? It was totally different from school.

"Hey, Michiko," I said. "Don't you think it would be better if she let us practice with the same utensils until we've remembered the *o-temae* completely, even if it does take three or four years?"

"Yeah, I do. I wonder why Sensei changes them every week?"

"If I was a Tea teacher, I'd definitely let my students use the same items until they'd mastered the basics."

I repeated the process twenty times, then twenty-five.

It was still as clear as mud to me three months later, when August came around and we had four weeks off Tea. During the summer holiday, I didn't touch my *fukusa* once. Michiko went overseas on a university trip, and had not yet returned when September arrived and our weekly lessons resumed.

Ugh, I'll probably have to start all over again . . .

It was still hot, so the walk to Sensei's home left me drenched in sweat.

The house had no air conditioning. All the doors were left open to ventilate the rooms. I could hear cars and bicycles passing by and the voices of people who had stopped to chat on the road outside. The garden resounded to the *chirp-click!* of cicadas.

I knelt before the kettle for the first time in a month.

"Bow. And take a breath. Now move the *kensui* forward. Grasp the tea bowl toward the front, then the *natsume*."

Listening to the same directions as before, I silently moved my hands. Sweat trickled down my back. My feet prickled and gradually went numb from kneeling.

*

A strange thing happened as I was coming to the end of the *o-temae*.

"Then move the *kensui* back . . ."

I pulled back the *kensui* full of waste water as instructed. The same hand then went automatically to my hip and took out my *fukusa*.

Oh!

My hand was moving of its own accord, before I could even think about what came next. The *hishaku* described an arc from *mizusashi* to kettle as though on invisible rails. After putting the lid back on the kettle, I shifted my gaze automatically to the *mizusashi*, which was still open. My hand instinctively stretched out toward the lid leaning against it.

Sensei nodded.

It was so sudden. My hands moved intuitively, without any thought involved. It was like being controlled by something else. But it felt great, somehow . . .

What could that strange sensation be?

In the *mizuya* the following week, Michiko—just back from her trip abroad—brought her slightly tanned face close to mine and whispered, "You didn't practice on your own during the summer vacation, did you, Nori?"

"Nope, not at all."

"Honest? I don't think I can even fold the *fukusa* anymore."

Looking apprehensive, she picked up the *mizusashi* and headed to the tea room. When she started her *o-temae,* it was my turn to be taken aback. No sooner had she poised the *hishaku* than her hand picked up her *fukusa* and used it to lift the lid from the kettle, as if it knew what it was doing itself. I watched her hand scoop hot water into the bowl with the *hishaku* and reach for the *chasen*.

"Good!"

Precisely repeating small, individual gestures is like drawing tiny dots. As these dots multiply, they gradually become lines. Some of these lines were finally beginning to form in our *o-temae*.

"Trust Your Hands"

However, we still could not seem to connect everything into a single smooth line. The flow frequently broke in the middle of our *o-temae,* and a slight exclamation would escape our lips as we were pierced by sudden uncertainty. When assailed by doubt for a moment, I would instantly start to think, *Ummm . . . Like this, then like that . . .*

But, with a shake of her head, Takeda-sensei would say, "No, stop thinking. You're always too quick to start thinking. You mustn't think with your head. Your hands know what to do. Try listening to them."

Listen to my hands?!

Eventually, though, there came a day when I was somehow able to perform the whole *o-temae* smoothly. I still don't really understand how I did it. But I got through to the end so naturally and effortlessly that it was almost anticlimactic.

Takeda-sensei smiled broadly.

"See, you don't need to think with your head. Just trust your hands."

CHAPTER 3

Focus Your Feelings on the Now

An Unexpected Change

Just as our *o-temae* started to connect into a single unbroken line, the day came when we unexpectedly had to change it again.

It was November, six months after we had begun learning Tea. Entering the tea room as usual for our lesson, we stopped short. The room looked different.

There was what I can only call a hole in the floor. A square of tatami had been cut out, about the size of a chessboard, and a black frame sat snugly within the edges. It was like a much smaller version of the sunken hearths you saw in old farmhouses. White steam rose from a kettle submerged up to its shoulders inside.

Michiko and I were still staring at the empty space that had suddenly appeared in the floor when we heard Takeda-sensei say, "Right then! From today, it's *ro*."

That box-shaped hole was called a *ro*. Hollowed out under the tea room floor, it had been there the whole time. In summer, it is hidden by an ordinary tatami mat, but in early November, which marks *rittō*—the beginning of winter in the traditional Japanese calendar—the mat is replaced with another that has a square cut out to reveal the *ro* beneath.

"The opening of the *ro* is called *robiraki*. It's often described as New Year for *chajin*." Sensei was in high spirits. The atmosphere in the room was more intense than ever.

The New Year? But it's only November!

30

In the *mizuya*, the utensils laid out for us also seemed vaguely different. The tea bowl was deeper, with thicker walls and a smaller mouth.

"To keep the water hot in the coldest depths of winter, we use a deep, narrow-mouthed tea bowl called a *tsutsu-jawan*."

I thought back to the height of summer, when we had used a shallow, wide-mouthed bowl called a *hira-jawan,* shaped like an upturned old-fashioned lampshade.

"So, let's get started with your *o-temae*."

"Yes, Sensei," we chorused, bowing.

I walked across the tatami in the usual way and knelt in the usual spot. I raised the *hishaku* slightly from its perch atop the *kensui* and lifted the bamboo *futaoki* out of the empty waste water bowl. (A *futaoki* is a stand a couple of inches high on which the kettle lid or *hishaku* rests during the procedure.) Just as I was about to put the *futaoki* down in its usual place, Takeda-sensei exclaimed, "Stop! Now, turn around toward the *ro*, just as you are."

"Sorry?"

"Keep hold of the *futaoki* and move around toward me so that you're facing this direction," she said, pointing at one corner of the *ro*.

I turned around as instructed and ended up kneeling diagonally across the tatami mat. There was something uncomfortably ambivalent about this forty-five-degree angle, facing neither straight ahead nor to the side.

"It's *ro*, so you do your *o-temae* sitting at this angle."

And that was just the beginning.

"It's *ro*, so you place the *futaoki* over here."

"Ah—it's *ro*, so you line up the tea container and *chasen* over there."

"It's *ro*, so you put the tea bowl out for the guest here."

The layout of the utensils had completely changed. Things were not where they should have been. I was constantly looking around. Everything had been transformed and I was in a total muddle.

I started to say, "Sensei, in the *o-temae* I did before—"

Takeda-sensei cut me off. "That. Was. Summer. Tea. This. Is. Winter. Tea," she said, emphasizing each word with a chop of one hand against the other.

"You mean, the summer and winter *o-temae* are different?"

"Yes."

"So, the *o-temae* we learned up till now . . ."

"Never mind all that. Forget about summer *o-temae*."

I was dumbfounded by her words.

I could not believe that we had been corrected on every little thing and repeated the procedure dozens of times, only for her to turn around and tell us to forget it just as we were getting the hang of things. Everything that we had been working on had been demolished. All our efforts had been in vain. My mind was in utter disarray.

Why won't she just let us do the same o-temae all year round?!

*

"You've got to put it behind you and move on. When it's *ro* season, you focus on *ro o-temae*."

Despite my doubts and confusion, I would be doing winter Tea whether I liked it or not.

Winter Tea

And so I started from zero again. Following Sensei's orders, I moved utensils from right to left, scooped hot water, and opened and closed lids.

"Turn the *hishaku* face-down and lower it into the mouth of the kettle . . . No, don't suspend it on the lip—the cup of the ladle goes inside the mouth."

"Dear me, is the stem of that *hishaku* one-third of the way along the hearth frame?"

"What are you looking at? The *chakin*'s over here."

The torrent of corrections and procedures, all different from summer Tea, seemed never-ending. I struggled to keep up. Everything from earlier in the year vanished from my memory. That was the only way I could do what I needed to now.

I simply repeated the process as directed—five times, ten, fifteen.

As Michiko and I walked home side by side in our coats and gloves, our words came out in white clouds of steam.

"I made a lot of mistakes again today."

"Me too. I was all over the place."

*

33

While this was going on, I started to think about skipping Tea when Saturdays came around. But, despite my reluctance, I turned up each week to find new utensils awaiting us in the kerosene-stove-heated *mizuya*.

"This is a *hira-natsume*. It's wide and flat, so you place it in the palm of your hand like this to wipe it."

"You wipe the narrow *tsutsu-jawan* like this."

"With this kind of *tana*, the first thing you do after kneeling is take out the metal charcoal chopsticks."

Not again!

Utensils and *tana* that we had never seen before made their appearance, in endless succession. They were tricky to use, so I made mistakes. Determined not to get it wrong, I would immerse myself in my *o-temae*, and a few seconds of thought-free emptiness would spontaneously come to me. When that happened, I felt fleetingly, pleasantly detached from everything. Those were the days I returned home refreshed, my earlier half-heartedness entirely forgotten.

My initial discomfort about sitting at an angle had vanished. I no longer looked wildly around me to find things that should have been there but were not, or put my hand out for something only to withdraw it again after remembering where the item actually was. Once the winter procedure had sunk in, it all seemed normal.

After finishing an *o-temae*, the rush of cold air from the hallway when I opened the sliding paper screen made me wince. I realized for the first time that winter how much insulation a thin paper screen could provide.

Summer Tea

A whole year had passed since Michiko and I had started learning Tea. We were now fourth-years at university. The cherry blossoms scattered and new leaves appeared on the trees, glowing an almost luminous green. Sweaters were no longer needed. During the Golden Week vacation, I took a trip with classmates from my graduation thesis class, while Michiko returned home to visit her parents.

When we turned up to our first Tea lesson after the string of holidays, the *ro* had disappeared. In early May—the season called *rikka*, which marks the start of summer in the old calendar—the *ro* is closed up and the tatami mats changed again.

"Well then, today we start doing summer Tea, so we're back to the *furo*."

In a corner of the room, the kettle sat on a brazier—the *furo*. With the glow of the charcoal hidden from view, the warmth of the fire seemed a long way away.

But while the fire was further from us, the cold water was closer. A flat, sunflower-yellow *mizusashi* with a wide mouth squatted imposingly on the tatami.

"Let's get started, then."

"Yes, Sensei," we replied, bowing.

I removed the *futaoki* from the *kensui* as usual, then turned forty-five degrees—and froze. Of course, there was no *ro* anymore.

35

"So which direction do you face? You've forgotten, haven't you?" Sensei chuckled.

My mind was a blank. I could not recall any of what I had done just six months earlier.

"Sit facing front. You put the *futaoki* in that little gap beside the kettle, remember? Place the *hishaku* on it and then bow. Right, now take a breath . . . and move the *kensui* forward."

Moving awkwardly, robotically, in response to each and every instruction, I felt as if I was doing everything for the first time. We were back at square one again. Once more, I was thrown into turmoil by a combination of despondency that none of what I had learned half a year ago had remained and reluctance to abandon the *ro* procedure now that I was finally familiar with it.

Why won't she just let us do the same thing the whole time?!

It seemed like the Buddhist legend of the *Sai no Kawara*, where dead children are condemned to the Sisyphean task of building small stone towers, only to have them destroyed time and again.

Perhaps sensing my consternation, Takeda-sensei said, "In *furo* season, do the *furo* procedure. Forget about the *ro* procedure."

She never let us stand still. Clinging to the past was not allowed.

"Come now, you've got to move on. Take care of what's in front of you. You've got to focus your feelings on the now."

CHAPTER 4

Watch and Feel

Host and Guest

Michiko and I always took turns playing host and guest. The host would make tea and the guest would drink it. When I was the host, I strained every sinew to avoid mistakes in my *o-temae,* but as soon as I switched to being the guest, all feelings of tension were swept away in a wave of relief.

While I was eating my sweet and waiting absently for the tea to be served, Takeda-sensei gently chided me: "Come on, now. Pay attention to your host's *o-temae.*"

Michiko was intently purifying the tea whisk in the process called *chasen-tōshi,* rotating and lifting the whisk to check that none of the fine bamboo prongs were broken. The fingers of her right hand were neatly aligned, forming a straight line that ran all the way to her raised elbow.

Holding the tea bowl level, she draped the white *chakin* over the rim to wipe both sides, her slim wrists flexing deftly as she gave the bowl three generous turns. Although she was performing the same procedure as I had, her earnest character was curiously evident in each movement.

"You see," said Sensei, "watching someone else's *o-temae,* you feel all kinds of things. Sometimes you'll be struck by the elegance of a particular movement. Watching and feeling are an important part of learning Tea."

Come to think of it, we had never seen Takeda-sensei's own *o-temae.*

She had made tea for us on the first day, but we knew nothing about *o-temae* back then, so we had no idea what was what. I remembered watching it as a single sequence of movements, like a dance.

When we first learned a particular technique like *fukusa-sabaki* or *chasen-tōshi*, Sensei patiently showed us each movement. However, after that, she taught with words alone.

It was January before we saw Takeda-sensei's *o-temae* again, when all her students gathered for *Hatsugama*.

Hatsugama

Hatsugama is the first Tea lesson of the New Year, but it does not actually involve practicing *o-temae* like a normal lesson. Instead, students pay their respects for the New Year to their teacher, who lays on a meal of the *o-sechi* delicacies traditional at the start of the year before performing *o-temae* for the assembled students. This ceremony marks the start of Tea lessons again after the New Year's holiday.

Dressed in kimono for the first time, Michiko and I made our way to Sensei's house together a little before noon. When we opened the door to the entrance hall and called, "Hello!" as usual, nothing but a profound silence answered from within. Several pairs of *zōri*—the split-toe sandals worn with kimono— were lined up on the water-sprinkled floor.

The five housewives who Takeda-sensei taught on Wednesdays were already there. We heard a murmur of voices, and then a middle-aged woman in a celadon-green kimono bound with a golden-brown obi peeked out at us and bowed slightly. We unconsciously stiffened in the face of this unfamiliar air of grown-up formality.

Prepared for *Hatsugama,* the tea room was as fresh and bright as a crisp white sheet. Hanging from the pillar of the *tokonoma* alcove was a vase of green bamboo in which two camellia buds had been arranged, one red and one white. Long willow branches also cascaded out in a big loop and trailed almost to the floor. On the scroll, I could make out characters meaning "crane dance" and "one thousand years." Three small golden-yellow bales of rice were stacked on an unvarnished wooden stand in the very center of the *tokonoma.*

So this is the real Japanese New Year . . .

I glanced over to where I usually did *o-temae* and found myself captivated by the tea utensils on display. There was a large, elegant, two-legged *tana.* The gold and black lacquer of the *robuchi* framing the hearth and the jet-black *natsume* gleamed lustrously in the pure, white winter light.

There's something so sophisticated about the black of lacquerware!

The milky white *mizusashi* had a turquoise crane painted on it.

Tiny pine cones adorned the top of the metal charcoal chopsticks.

I had always assumed tradition to be stale and boring, but I had been wrong. Real traditions were modern and innovative. In that moment, I perceived Japan as an exotic country, as if seeing through the eyes of the French who had so admired *japonisme* a century before.

Looking comfortable in a single-crested pale cream kimono with a design on the skirt, Takeda-sensei placed both hands on the tatami and said, "Happy New Year, everyone. I look forward to teaching you all again this year. Please continue to pursue your studies diligently."

We placed our fans before us and chorused, "Happy New Year, Sensei," then raised our heads as one.

The formal greetings completed, Sensei announced, "Now then, I shall do *o-temae*. Do be sure to watch closely, because even I make mistakes. I usually correct you on your *o-temae*, but I have to confess that it's all talk. I'm not very good at actually doing it myself."

Laughter rippled across the room, lightening the atmosphere in an instant. With that, Sensei disappeared into the *mizuya*.

Sensei's Bow

Seven students silently awaited Takeda-sensei's reappearance.

At *Hatsugama*, Sensei always performed *koicha-temae*— the procedure for making thick tea. If *usucha*—thin tea—is the *matcha* equivalent of cappuccino, then *koicha* could be likened to espresso. The type of *matcha* used differs and the *o-temae* itself is more advanced. In the case of *usucha*, one bowl is made for each guest, whereas *koicha* requires enough tea for several guests to be kneaded with the *chasen* in a single bowl, which is passed around for everyone to drink a few sips.

The paper screen slid back.

Kneeling at the threshold, Sensei placed her hands together in front of her knees, looked steadily at her gathered students, and then gracefully lowered her head. Just as it seemed that she had paused for a moment, she gradually raised it again.

It was as simple as that. Yet it pierced my heart.

She had resembled a bird crouching with flattened feathers for a second before fluffing them back up again. Sensei had just demonstrated her respect for us. Modestly, humbly, but without a trace of subservience. A bow was not merely the act of lowering the head. The simple gesture of bowing contained . . . a world of meaning. The form *was* the spirit. Or rather, the spirit had taken form.

Oh, that's what she meant . . .

I had seen Takeda-sensei bow any number of times by that point, but only then did I understand my mother's remark about her bow being different from everyone else's.

Sensei's *Koicha-temae*

Carrying two stacked tea bowls, one coated with gold on the inside and the other with silver, Sensei stood up straight and tall, then began to walk. Her feet slid softly over the tatami mats, never leaving the surface. As I watched her white split-toe *tabi* socks, I was reminded of a Noh actor's gait as they step across the stage.

With everyone gazing on wordlessly, Sensei slowly took a breath before beginning her *o-temae*.

She moved the *kensui* forward, placed the tea bowl in front of her, and carried out all the same movements that she usually directed us to perform. She placed a beautiful brocade bag holding the *chaire*—the ceramic container for thick tea—before her knees, and delicately untied the knotted cord.

Although Sensei's hands were as chapped from cooking and cleaning as any other housewife's, her fingers moved smoothly, each digit seemingly guided by its own instinct. She loosened the mouth of the bag, exposed the shoulders of the *chaire*—right, left—and carefully took it out, handling the container with infinite care. It was as though she were undressing someone.

Her *fukusa-sabaki* was slow and deliberate, with a kind of delicate rhythm.

While exactly the same size as ours and made of the same fabric, the tightly folded *fukusa* in Sensei's hand somehow looked as fluffy as a soufflé. Using the soft fold of the cloth, Sensei drew a small *ko* as she wiped the *chaire*'s lid, and then paused for a beat at its shoulder before stroking the *fukusa* down the side of the container. Her movements were gentle. Each one had an indescribable roundness to it that never faltered.

Amid the silence, everyone's eyes were riveted on Sensei's hands, for fear of missing a single detail. But no matter how hard we looked, there was no sign that she was adding any special movements.

She was simply carrying out the procedure in the way that she always taught us, naturally and unhesitatingly, without any mannerisms or showy gestures, and without abbreviating or altering anything.

What on earth made such a difference, then?

The water that bubbles up from pure mountain springs is glass-clear, with no smells or peculiar flavors. It slips down your throat smoothly and soaks right into your body. Nothing is added and nothing removed.

Takeda-sensei's *o-temae* was just like that spring water. It was slow and stately in some places, light and brisk in others. The flow was punctuated at certain points by the soft *pock!* of the *hishaku* or *chink!* of the *chasen* being set down.

Sensei poured hot water over the *koicha* and began to knead it with the *chasen*. Her movements were unhurried to start with as she blended the tea with the hot water. Soon the strokes of the *chasen* became more rhythmical, occasionally breaking into a different cadence before returning to the first, gradually building to a peak. Finally, she drew the spiral of the hiragana character *no* and slowly lifted the *chasen* from the bowl.

A faint sigh escaped the lips of the assembled students.

Watching the movements of Sensei's hands felt good somehow. It was like listening to music with my eyes. Yet all she had done was pour hot water on the *matcha* and knead it, in a perfectly natural, ordinary way.

"Watch closely. Watching and feeling are also part of learning."

Just like Sensei had told us, it was not just about performing the procedure without making any mistakes. *O-temae* that followed the set procedure looked something like a favorite dress. But in Sensei's case, she was not simply wearing the dress. Rather, the dress had molded itself to her body.

CHAPTER 5

Look at Many
Real Things

Chakai

In March of the year after we had begun learning Tea, Sensei asked us, "How would you like to go to a *chakai*? There's one coming up—perhaps you'd like to go on a study outing for a change?"

"A *chakai*! Really?"

On our way home that day, Michiko and I let our imaginations run wild, excited by what we thought would be the chance to see high society for ourselves at one of these tea gatherings.

"There's bound to be a red carpet and someone playing the *koto*."

"All those elegant ladies in kimono strolling through a Japanese garden. It'll be just like in *The Makioka Sisters*."

"I wonder if they'll laugh in that condescending way, like in the movies?"

"I bet there'll be a lot of women showing off to each other . . ."

"Almost certainly. They'll probably exchange catty remarks while smiling sweetly at one another."

"Gosh, it's like that movie slogan, 'Women only blossom when they're rivals.'"

The word *chakai* was enough to conjure up vulgar visions of glamorous hotbeds of snobbishness and spite. But at the same time, we realized that these images were too tacky to be true. The reality would probably be totally different.

*

On the day of the *chakai*, we got up uncharacteristically early and traveled with Sensei to Sankeien Garden in Yokohama's Honmoku district.

Chajin have to rise with the lark. A crowd had already gathered outside Sankeien by the time we arrived, even though the nine o'clock opening of the gates was still some time away. It seemed as though women in kimono had assembled there from every corner of Japan.

Almost all of them were middle-aged or elderly ladies. I saw only a couple of men, and they looked to be in their seventies. The few young women in their early twenties were all, like us, trailing in the wake of stately kimono-clad figures who must have been their teachers.

While we were waiting for the gate to open, the exchange of greetings between one sensei and another began. For some reason, they all spoke in hushed tones.

"My, my. You did get here early."

"Oh, hello. My, my, haven't we been fortunate with the weather?"

"You're quite right, the weather is the best treat of all."

Flurries of *my, my*'s—a rather strange interjection that was neither an exclamation of surprise nor a means of address—could be heard all around us.

"Which group do you plan to start with today?" said one lady to her companion.

"I'm not sure. If we don't get the order right, we won't be able to visit them all."

49

"Oh, all of them would be impossible. We definitely won't get to the ones we want unless you go and line up for the *koicha* session while I get our tickets for a later *usucha* session."

"My, my. Well then, let's do our best."

"My, my. I'll see you later, then."

The middle-aged ladies seemed positively giddy with enthusiasm. Takeda-sensei also appeared excited, cheerily exchanging *my, my*'s with other teachers with whom she was evidently friendly. Overwhelmed, Michiko and I observed from the sidelines.

The Long Line

Nine o'clock. The gate opened and the kimonoed women filed inside. We too marched along the gravel path like a line of ants and were drawn inexorably into the Inner Garden.

Sankeien is a vast Japanese garden built by a wealthy merchant in the early twentieth century. Dotted about its grounds is an assortment of old tea rooms of all sizes. This *chakai* had been organized by a group of Tea teachers who had hired the venue and were serving tea in five different rooms around the garden, one for each teacher. The small tea rooms could hold around fifteen people and the large rooms more than twenty. The first session in each of the five rooms would start at ten o'clock and last about half an hour, following which each host group would perform *o-temae* over and over again until about three in the afternoon.

You might think that we could have taken our time in arriving instead of getting up so early. However, the number of people was simply incredible. The corridors outside each tea room were jam-packed with ladies in kimono, and we took our place at the end of a line that already snaked back a long way by the time we arrived. The twenty people who had secured places for the first session must have made a mad dash through the corridors as they jockeyed to get there ahead of the pack.

There was no *koto* music. This was not high society. This situation, with women all lined up, reminded me of something entirely different. What could it be?

Oh, of course! The first day of a big department store sale!

The long corridor encircling the large room was chock-full of kimono-clad women lined up two by two. The queue stretched around one corner and then another. Having lagged behind, we were at about the halfway point and would have to wait more than an hour. From time to time, someone on their way to the toilet would wade through the crowd, saying, "Excuse me, please let me through!" This would turn the corridor into a sea of chaos.

With a wry smile, Takeda-sensei remarked, "Terrible, isn't it? You must be shocked. When I came to my first *chakai,* back in the day, some people even climbed out through the ornamental window amid the confusion. I was so disappointed to see *chajin* behaving like that!"

When preparations for the first session were complete, the sliding paper door opened and a woman in her twenties wearing a kimono in graduated shades of peach-pink bowed and said, "Please come in." The twenty people at the head of the line each bowed to the person behind them and offered the customary "Excuse me for going first" before disappearing into the tea room in turn, one at a time. Before long, the young woman in peach popped her head out of the door again and addressed the three people who were first in line for the next session: "We can seat another three people, so please come in."

"Oh dear," said the plump, bespectacled middle-aged woman at the front of the queue. "There are four in our group. Can't we all come in?" She was dressed in a visiting kimono with an ornate Tsujigahana tie-dyed design and a formal obi bearing a pattern of fans decorated with flowers and birds.

"I'm terribly sorry," the younger woman said, "I'm afraid we only have space for three."

"Well, that's no good. All four of us are together. Aren't we?" Through the oversized lenses of a pair of lavender glasses that made her look oddly like a certain male screenwriter who was something of a celebrity in those days, Tsujigahana exchanged glances with the other three in her entourage.

"That's right, we have to stay together."

"Yes, surely one more would be fine? We all came here together."

The young woman in peach did her best to resist, protesting that it would inconvenience the other guests, but Tsujigahana and her retinue stood up and barged their way in regardless, ignoring all attempts to dissuade them.

It brought to mind someone on an overcrowded train, wriggling their behind into a small gap to claim a seat. We heard someone inside the tea room say, "I'm terribly sorry, but would you mind moving up?" followed by a commotion as the other guests shuffled over to make space.

Ōyose Chakai

I saw this scene repeated at every *chakai* I subsequently attended. Large public tea gatherings like this are called *ōyose chakai* and they offer the chance to see people in all their infinite variety. One time, while I was waiting my turn in the corridor, I happened to overhear this conversation:

"Oh, that reminds me. I must reimburse you for the other day."

"Sensei, really, it's fine."

"No, no, I insist."

I could not keep my eyes from straying toward the source of the voices—a woman of around seventy and another in her forties who I took to be the older woman's pupil. The first woman took a wallet from her purse, whipped a sheet of *kaishi* (the paper on which sweets are placed) from the fold where the left and right sides of her azuki-colored unpatterned kimono crossed at the breast, and then rolled the money up in the paper, turning to the side to conceal her actions from her student. The movement of her hands somehow caught my eye. The teacher extracted a long, thin object from her purse and touched it to the corner of her mouth before withdrawing it again, quick as a flash. It was a lip brush, of all things.

Cap of the lip brush still in her mouth, the teacher hurriedly scribbled something on the improvised *kaishi* envelope, then put the cap back on the lip brush and returned it to her purse. She turned to her pupil and, voicing her thanks, proffered the small package with both hands.

I saw the characters indicative of a gift written, somewhat raspily, in red on the *kaishi* wrapper.

It was the first time I had ever thought of such an elderly woman as cool.

Another time, we were waiting near the front of the line when a member of the host group announced, "We can seat another three people—please come in."

Ahead of us in the queue was a woman in her sixties wearing a sophisticated olive-green kimono with a fine shark skin pattern, horizontal ribs of her heavy *shioze*-weave obi prominent on her *taiko* knot as she sat with her back to us. Now she removed her reading glasses, turned to us, and said, "Please go ahead. There are three of you, aren't there?"

"But . . ." If we jumped the queue, this lady would have to wait another half an hour.

"It's fine—I've brought a book."

She smiled as she showed us a small paperback book spread out on top of her expensive-looking camel lap blanket. I realized that she had been quietly reading all along. Perhaps finding the strain hard on her aging eyes, she would read a little and then gaze out at the garden for a while. She seemed to be cocooned in a world of her own, away from the hubbub of the queue in the corridor.

"Thank you so much. In that case, we'll take you up on your kind offer. Excuse us . . ." By the time we turned back at the tea room door to bow to her, she was looking down at her book again, back in her own little world.

The Role of the Main Guest

The shuffling sounds continued for a short while after Tsujigahana and her entourage forced their way into the tea room, but gradually subsided. Then a profound silence suddenly fell.

Oh, the o-temae *has started.*

Still in the corridor, I strained my ears. I could hear the rustle of a kimono and footsteps lightly grazing the tatami. The hush was broken by the *snap!* of *chiriuchi.*

At *ōyose chakai, o-temae* is performed not by the host teacher, but by their pupils. Two bowls of *usucha* are usually made. The first is drunk by the *shōkyaku,* or main guest, who sits at the head of the line of guests, and the second by their left-hand neighbor, the *jikyaku* or second guest. Then other pupils bring out *usucha* whisked in the *mizuya* for the rest of the guests, starting with the third and proceeding down the line.

The host teacher's job is to sit facing the row of guests and converse with the *shōkyaku.* She acts something like the hostess at a dinner party, ensuring that all the guests are enjoying themselves, while answering the *shōkyaku*'s questions about the calligraphy on the scroll, the flowers in the *tokonoma,* that day's utensils, and so on.

The main guest does more than just sit in the top seat and drink tea before everyone else. They have the important role of asking the questions that the other guests likely have for the host, and generally setting the mood in the room. This is precisely why there is an unspoken rule that the first guest should be a veteran *chajin,* with a wealth of knowledge and experience.

Battle of Humility

An hour later, our turn finally came.

"Sensei, where should we sit?"

"Anywhere but the main guest's place," Sensei replied. "Apart from that, just sit where you like."

The chaos that met our eyes when we entered the tea room resembled nothing so much as a battle for a seat on the train. I stuck close to Takeda-sensei, and Michiko to me, and before we knew it, the three of us were seated just over halfway down the line of guests.

The only spaces left were the two for the main guest and second guest, right at the head of the row. Nobody made a move to sit there. Still standing in the middle of the room were two flustered middle-aged ladies who had been late joining in this unique variation on musical chairs.

"There are places free here, so please take a seat." The attendant tried to usher them into the spaces for *shōkyaku* and *jikyaku,* but the two women became even more alarmed. Insisting, "Oh, we couldn't possibly. That wouldn't do at all!" they managed to wedge themselves hurriedly right into a spot where no gap had existed a moment earlier.

This meant that, little by little, everyone else had to shift sideways to relieve the squeeze. The third guest, who was closest to the top seat, appeared anxious lest she end up being pressed into the main guest's place. Her grim look revealed her determined not to budge from that spot at any cost, no matter how much she might be exhorted to move.

There was something comically infantile about the sight of these kimonoed middle-aged and elderly ladies jostling each other in the tea room like children playing some rough-and-tumble game.

"Could I possibly prevail upon one of you to be *shōkyaku*?"

Despite the host's entreaties, nobody stepped forward.

"We need someone to serve as main guest. Please."

You could have heard a pin drop. Time was the only thing that moved. Everyone seemed to have turned to stone.

"Please, somebody. Without a *shōkyaku*, we can't start the session!" Her voice had taken on an exasperated edge.

Someone spoke up: "—sensei, would you be so kind?" All eyes instantly turned to an elderly lady in a brown kimono tied with a black obi. It was settled.

"Oh, no, I really couldn't. It wouldn't do at all for me to sit in such a position of honor."

But despite the intense reluctance of the little old lady, the attendant dragged her and her companion by the hand to the *shōkyaku* and *jikyaku* spaces.

The grandmotherly figure who had become the main guest looked to be in her mid-eighties. Loath as she had been to take on the role, as soon as she lightly settled herself into the *shōkyaku* spot, she straightened the hem of her kimono, adjusted her collar, then placed her fan before her knees and beamed as she addressed us all: "My, my. Please do pardon me for taking such a lofty position. I'm looking forward to this chance to study today."

Once the *shōkyaku* vacancy had been filled, relief rippled through the room, the sardine-like squash eased, and everyone sat more comfortably.

Utensils

The *o-temae* got underway. A woman of about twenty, holding a tea bowl and *natsume*, entered the room, which was lined with precious sliding-screen paintings. Her cheeks were flushed, probably with nervousness, but her demeanor as she carried out her *o-temae* was serene.

Everybody's eyes were glued to her hands. I heard faint whispers:

"I wonder if that *natsume*'s a Kinsa?"

"There's a *kaō* on the folding screen."

"Isn't that hearth frame with the budding willow design lovely? It's a Sōtetsu."

Michiko and I had not the faintest idea what they were talking about.

The greetings between host and main guest began.

"My, my. I must offer my congratulations to you," said the *shōkyaku*.

"My, my. Thank you for coming," replied the host.

"Aren't we fortunate that it's so much warmer today?"

"That's a treat in itself."

"Sensei, these are such superb utensils! It's very thoughtful of you, but the preparations must have been terribly hard work."

"It's not much, but we've done what we could."

Then the main guest inquired about each utensil in turn, giving the host her chance to explain. "This one was made by twelfth-generation Raku master Kōnyū. Grand Master Sokuchūsai bestowed it with the name 'Spring haze' . . . That one, with the design of flowers and grasses, is by Eiraku Zengorō . . . The *natsume* is 'Spring field' by Kinsa . . . The *chashaku* is . . ."

I've never been comfortable with the menus at French restaurants. Descriptions like "Duck foie gras charlotte with pepper caramel sauce and Sauternes granite" are all Greek to me. This was just the same. Sakakura Shinbei, Ōhi Chōzaemon, favored by Seisai, favored by Sokuchūsai, box inscription . . . on and on it went. It was some time before I learned that *sometsuke* was a type of blue and white pottery, glossy plain black lacquer was called *shin-nuri*, and *maki-e* was a technique for decorating lacquerware with silver and gold powder.

Now and then, the main guest would interject with "Oh, how splendid! It has a *kaō*," commenting on an item bearing the signature of a grand master, or "What a magnificent . . ." or "Such characteristic attention to detail . . ." or some other such comment.

Here and there, I heard eager exclamations from the other guests: "Goodness! The box is inscribed by Sokuchūsai?" "She says it's a Kōnyū. How wonderful!" The row of observers grew excited, the words "box" and *"kaō"* echoing around the room and names like Shinbei and Chōzaemon, redolent of a period drama, tripping off their tongues.

This was a totally different world from Tea as we knew it in our weekly lessons. Michiko and I could only look on, dumbfounded.

Haiken

Just as I had finished my *usucha*, the tea bowl that each guest had carefully examined in the process called *haiken* came round to us. It was black and glossy. Sensei bent down low and looked long and hard at the bowl. Then she firmly cupped both hands around it and placed it gently in front of me.

"This is a Raku tea bowl. Make sure you actually touch it while examining it," she instructed. "Feel the weight, the texture, how it fits into your hands. Then turn it over and take a good look, because you'll see the Raku seal impressed into the base.

You have to study the details of the seals so that you can tell which generation of the Raku family made it."

"I see."

The *haiken* process as carried out by the matronly ladies around me was nothing short of astounding. Placing both hands on the tatami, they steadily gazed at the bowl, then folded both hands around it and turned it as they felt its weight and finish. Some lifted their glasses up while peering at the inside, the impression of the Raku seal on the underside, and the bottom rim or "foot" of the bowl. They subjected it to intense scrutiny, as if lapping up every little detail, inside and out.

I was a little embarrassed to stare at someone's possession as if appraising it, but I did as I was told.

The tea bowl was as soft and light as a meringue. When I picked it up, it had a kind of warmth to it, nestling snugly in my hands like a small animal. Any awkwardness about appearing to be evaluating the bowl evaporated as soon as I savored its texture with my palms.

It was only several years later that I discovered that that tea bowl had been worth several million yen.

Sensei told us, "When you come to a *chakai,* you must make sure to touch the utensils like that. You need to look at many real things with your own eyes. Watch how the different main guests and hosts act. That's how you gain experience—how you learn."

*

The *o-temae* finished and the *natsume* and *chashaku* were laid out on the tatami. The host and guest exchanged closing salutations. We all placed our fans in front of us and bowed. No sooner had we done so than the middle-aged women all rushed forward. I wondered what on earth had happened.

Everyone was clustered round the utensils in a crowd several deep, opening the *natsume* to look at the underside of the lid and picking up the *chashaku*.

"It's a lovely *chashaku*, isn't it?"

"My word, this hearth frame is fabulous!"

Nichinichi Kore Kōjitsu

I discovered only one thing I recognized at that day's *chakai*. It was the scroll:

Nichinichi kore kōjitsu

The framed piece of calligraphy in Sensei's tea room bore the same text.

"Look at that!" I exclaimed.

"Oh, you're right! It's the same as the one at Sensei's place."

We gazed at the familiar five characters.

"Nori, what does it mean?" asked Michiko.

"Well, *kōjitsu* means 'good day,' doesn't it?"

"So . . . ?"

"So it means 'Every day is a good day,' right?"

"Even I know that! But is that all?"

"Huh? What do you mean, 'Is that all?'"

Sitting beside us, Sensei had been listening silently to this exchange. Now she chuckled.

Michiko appeared distinctly unconvinced by my explanation. I really had no idea what she was getting at. Surely "Every day is a good day" just means "Every day is a good day"? What other meaning could it possibly have?

I would spot that five-character phrase in other places after that.

Studying

The *chakai* included a boxed lunch called *tenshin*. A little after noon, Sensei took us to a large formal room set aside for lunch and we gazed out at the garden while we opened up our boxes of sushi.

Just then, an elderly lady addressed Sensei. "Oh, Mrs. Takeda, have you brought your young pupils with you today?"

She stood simply, wearing a bright gray single-crested kimono that perfectly complemented her neatly coiffed pearl-white hair and holding a pale violet shawl that looked soft as a cloud. She reminded me of a narcissus. The graceful young lady that she had once been still lived on inside her. I think she must have been over eighty, but she did not seem old. Amid the droves of attendees in their cliques, making a big deal about being "all four together," she was strolling around on her own. I had never seen anyone so beautiful.

I gazed at her, thinking, *I want to be like her someday*.

Sensei's acquaintance continued, "Are you about to have your lunch? I've just had mine." Then she gave a charming smile and took her leave: "Well, I'm off to study another session. Studying is so much fun, isn't it? Do excuse me for leaving before you . . ."

As I watched her depart, soft-looking pastel-hued shawl wrapped lightly about her shoulders, one particular word remained with me, disrupting the flow of my thoughts like a rock in the middle of a stream. Pausing with a piece of sushi halfway to my mouth, I said to Michiko, "That lady said 'studying,' didn't she?"

"Yes, she did . . ."

"I wonder why someone would still be studying at her age?"

"I wonder . . ."

Having finally been freed from examination hell upon entering university, the idea mystified us, but we heard the word "study" several times at the *chakai* that day. Sensei's acquaintance had used it, and so had the elderly teacher who had been the main guest at the first *o-temae* we attended that morning.

Listening to our conversation, Sensei chuckled to herself again.

CHAPTER 6

Savor the Seasons

THE WISDOM OF TEA

Reasons to Skip Lessons

Two years had passed since Michiko and I had started to learn Tea.

We had both graduated from university. I was working part-time for a publisher, while Michiko had found a job at a trading company.

It was no longer just the two of us at our weekly lessons. We had been joined by a third-year university student named Yumiko, a high school senior called Sanae, and a policewoman named Mrs. Tadokoro. On Saturdays, the tea room became a lively place.

Sensei went back to teaching the basics.

"Yes, now *chiriuchi*."

and

"Drape the *chakin* over the rim and give the bowl three good turns as you wipe."

Michiko and I could not suppress our giggles at the sight of the new students tiptoeing across the tatami.

After every lesson, the new students had to use their hands to wiggle their benumbed toes back and forth. Groaning at the intense tingling as the sensation returned to their feet, they exclaimed, "Ugh, I really don't have a clue what I'm doing!" and "Unbelievable! Are all those tiny little details really set in stone?"

"You must feel like you're watching your former selves," Sensei said.

Michiko and I laughed and nodded, but our own grasp of the details was still hazy, even in our third year of study.

We had learned *koicha o-temae,* and each week we were taught how to handle different forms of *mizusashi, tana* large and small, and a paulownia wood box called a *satsūbako*—not to mention the *sumi-temae* procedures for laying and replenishing the charcoal.

Sensei's instructions became more elaborate as the *o-temae* grew in length and complexity.

"Yes, starting with your right thumb, move your fingers in sequence, one by one . . . Now the fingers of your left hand. Then your right hand goes up and your left comes down . . ."

and

"When adding the charcoal on this side, you have to turn the hand holding the metal chopsticks away from the guests."

and

"Dear me, what about wiping the lid of the *mizusashi*?"

We confused the *usucha o-temae* with the *koicha* and were even more muddled than before, making the same mistakes over and over.

Even though we had been doing it more than two years, we made mistakes every time and got scolded every time. Sensei chided us, saying, "Come on now, this isn't your first time. Is this what I get in return for everything I've taught you? If this is how you're going to repay me, you might as well not bother."

and

"Oh, good heavens, have you forgotten that too? I'm too cross for words!"

I'm too cross for words: we heard that one a lot.

O-temae was waiting for us each time we went to our lesson. And when we did it, we always made mistakes, inevitably resulting in the rebuke "It's not your first time" or "I'm too cross for words!"

On Saturday afternoons, if it was raining, I would think, *I don't want to go to Tea in this weather.* If the weather was fine, though, the thought would be *I don't want to waste such a lovely Saturday doing Tea.*

There was always a reason to skip our lesson. I would dither about whether to go and then drag my heels all the way there even though I was already late. But when I got there, my mood invariably changed and I would be glad I had gone after all.

This was because something was always waiting for me in Takeda-sensei's tea room.

Wagashi

In the garden, the wisteria blossoms swayed. The light was dazzling as it shone through the young persimmon leaves, and a fresh breeze stirred the air from time to time.

Sensei told us, "Today, I have some nice cold *hatsu-gatsuo.* I'll just go and slice it," and bustled off to the kitchen.

We all exchanged puzzled glances. I wondered if Sensei was going to treat us to bonito sashimi. After all, it was the right season for that famous haiku about the joys of early summer:

Me ni wa aoba
    Yama hototogisu
        Hatsu-gatsuo
Looking at green leaves
    Hearing the mountain cuckoo
        First bonito—yum!

But I'd never heard of sashimi being paired with *matcha*.

When Sensei reappeared, she was carrying not sashimi plates and a soy sauce dispenser, but a lidded sweet dish.

Huh? But didn't Sensei say hatsu-gatsuo—*the first bonito of the year?*

"Please pass it around."

It seemed that she had thoughtfully chilled the Seto ware dish and its contents in the refrigerator, as it was pleasantly cool to the touch in the summer heat.

I lifted the lid to find slices of pale pink steamed *yōkan* lined up inside.

"This is *Hatsu-gatsuo* from the sweet shop Minochū in Nagoya," said Sensei.

"You mean, *Hatsu-gatsuo* is a sweet?"

"Were you expecting actual fish? Oh, how funny! Come on, now, take a piece."

But why do they call steamed yōkan *Hatsu-gatsuo?*

Using the spicewood chopsticks, I placed a slice on my *kaishi*. "Oh!" I cried. A pattern of stripes ran across the cut surface of the soft, yielding, pink confection. The color and pattern really did make it resemble a fillet of early bonito. "It looks just like it!"

"Doesn't it?" Sensei's eyes crinkled happily.

The mixture of bean jelly blended with plenty of arrowroot is stirred only once during the steaming process before being chilled and left to set. When it is sliced with a taut thread, the cut surface takes on its distinctive striped texture.

Seeing the cut edge of the delicate pink sweet instantly rekindled memories of sitting around a small dining table with my family, eating fish in season. I almost caught a whiff of the aroma drifting past my nose.

With my sweet pick—not entirely unlike a very small, blunt knife—I cut the jelly into pieces and ate it, savoring the cool sensation on my tongue as it melted like ambrosia. The heady mixture of memories and sweetness was enchanting.

I loved mille-feuille and cream puffs, and had never taken any notice of *wagashi*—traditional Japanese confectionery—until starting to learn Tea. But within a year or two, my eyes had been opened to its charms.

Kinton—a variety of *wagashi* made from pureed beans colored and passed through a sieve to create fine flakes, which are then carefully applied to a small ball of bean paste—has many faces, portraying canola flowers in March, cherry blossom in April, and azaleas in May. In summer, arrowroot and agar are used to represent water, providing a sense of coolness. *Wagashi* are flavored not simply with their ingredients, but with the season itself.

Cream puffs and cakes, which are always the same, all year round, came to seem boring in comparison.

Tasting

One day in mid-December, when a cold wind was blowing, small yellow *manjū* were arranged on the lacquer sweet dish.

"I dashed up to Nihonbashi to buy some sweets this morning," said Sensei.

On occasion, Sensei would take an hour-long train ride just to buy sweets for our lesson. She might go to Kuya in Ginza for yellow, gourd-shaped *Kimihyō*, or to Shiono in Akasaka for *Chiyogiku*, painstakingly carved to depict a chrysanthemum, or to Komaki in Kita-Kamakura for *Aoume*, which looked just like green plums.

"These are yuzu *manjū* from Nagato," she explained.

Of course—it was almost the winter solstice. They say that if you float yuzu in your bath on the solstice, which marks the start of midwinter, the lemon-like fruit will warm up your body and protect you from colds all year long.

We were captivated by the sight of those bright yellow buns. Unlike the smooth surface of an ordinary *manjū*, the outer layer was pitted and dimpled, just like real yuzu peel. In a slight hollow at the top was the tiny green nub of the calyx. This was crafted from green *nerikiri*, a dough made from white bean paste and glutinous rice flour.

Everyone goggled in wonder.

"Wow, haven't they done a good job?"

"I wonder how they made all those teeny holes on the skin?"

"Go ahead and try it," Sensei told us. "Make sure you really taste the flavor."

With the first bite, the citrussy flavor of yuzu filled my mouth. Real yuzu peel had been coarsely grated and mixed into the outer layer of the *manjū* to recreate the fruit's distinctive bumpy texture. *Incredible!*

I never failed to be amazed by the artistic tricks hidden within dainty Japanese sweets.

Sensei ordered seasonal *wagashi* from venerable sweet shops the length and breadth of Japan. From Hasegawa Ryūshiken in Fukui came *Fuku wa Uchi,* shaped like goddess of good fortune Otafuku's smiling face, to mark the casting out of evil spirits at the end of winter in February. From Shimane, Saneidō's *Natane no Sato,* reminiscent of spring butterflies fluttering over a canola blossom field. From Shōkadō in Aichi, there were the tiny, colorful, stardust-like cubes of *Hoshi no Shizuku.* From Kyoto, Kameya Norikatsu's *Hamazuto*—a clam shell that opens up to reveal a single savory miso bean encased in amber agar—provided a moment of respite from the fierce heat of August. *Miso Matsukaze* was another Kyoto confection, a miso-flavored sponge cake from Matsuya Tokiwa. And from Gorōmaruya in Toyama would come shards of *Usugōri,* resembling a thin layer of ice on a wintertide rice paddy.

*

"These are *Koshi no Yuki*. I ordered them from Yamatoya in Nagaoka, all the way up in Niigata Prefecture," said Sensei, one cold, gloomy Saturday in January.

Lined up on the tray were a handful of dry sweets, white and square like flattened sugar cubes. They did not appear to differ greatly from *rakugan,* a hard candy made from fine sugar.

Wondering why Sensei had gone to the trouble of ordering them from such a long way away, I placed one on my *kaishi,* then picked it up with my fingers and popped it into my mouth. Barely had I bitten into that white sweet than it slowly, softly began to dissolve on my tongue.

Letting out a muffled exclamation of surprise, I realized why these sweets were named, literally, "Snows of Koshi Province."

It's snow! This is snow!

I marveled at the sensation as the confection crumbled in my mouth. The snow melted away, leaving behind nothing but a faint sweetness.

The Drama of Tea Utensils

Until starting to learn Tea, I had mostly thought of its utensils in terms of old, plain, muddy-colored tea bowls and assumed that the oft-used term *"wabi-sabi"*—sometimes described as elegant simplicity—signified an incomprehensible, austere aesthetic that revered such things.

However, the reality was very different.

You might open an incense container shaped like a simple white plum flower to find it painted scarlet inside, suddenly transforming it into a red blossom. Fitting the lid of one plain black *usucha* container might reveal a wave pattern traced in gold on its underside. Or the dark lacquer of another *natsume* might, at first glance, appear to be unadorned, but on much closer scrutiny turn out to be engraved all over with a motif of *sakura* in full bloom bearing the name "Cherry Blossom at Night."

Tea utensils were incredibly stylish, even witty. They might look old-fashioned, but have an amusing name; or appear nothing special, but turn out to be elaborately decorated in one tiny corner. They usually possessed some surprising twist that lay in wait, ready to take your breath away.

Giving us the opportunity to puzzle out these little artifices and discover an appreciation of the season was Takeda-sensei's way of demonstrating her hospitality toward us. Every week, Sensei prepared this unusual form of entertainment, as if setting riddles. "I wonder how many you'll get today," she would say.

Names of Flowers

"Do you know what today's flowers are?"

Prompted by Sensei's question, I looked over at the *tokonoma* and saw a bamboo basket. In it stood two or three flowers and long, slender stems of grass, an oasis of coolness in the sticky rainy season.

There were always flowers on display in the *tokonoma*. Unlike the grand floral displays at a party or bizarre *ikebana* arrangements in which flowers are impaled on the spikes of a metal frog like so many *objets d'art,* the flowers in the tea room's alcove were always simple and unostentatiously arranged, whether a single camellia bud in a long-necked, narrow-mouthed vase or a collection of wispy grasses and wild flowers in a basket.

"No," I admitted. "What are they called?"

"That tall, tapered one like a chopstick is called *kugaisō.* The pink one is a maiden lily. And that's reed canary grass." Sensei even knew the names of grasses that looked like weeds.

The following Saturday it was "False-buck's-beard, Japanese meadowsweet, and linden viburnum."

And the next time, "This is rose of Sharon and that's maiden hair grass." We would hear new names every week and return the following week to find more unfamiliar flowers waiting for us.

I had always liked flowers, starting with the daffodils, violets, and lily of the valley in our little flowerbed at home, as well as winter daphne, gardenia, and orange-flowered osmanthus in the park. Goldband lilies, plumed thistles, and spotted bellflowers on the embankments. Daisy fleabane, Oriental lady's thumb, Japanese lady bell in the fields . . . The names of all these flowers had been familiar to me since childhood.

But I was a stranger to the blooms in the tea room. This was an entirely different world, not available from just any florist. They even had their own name: *chabana,* or "flowers for Tea."

Where on earth did such flowers bloom?

"They mostly grow in our garden," Sensei told us.

"Really? This house's garden?"

For thirty years or so, Sensei had been transplanting flowers and grasses from various places and carefully tending to them.

From the tea room, we could see large persimmon and plum trees, along with azalea, wisteria, a grapevine, flowering quince, camellia, crepe myrtle, peach, hydrangea, heavenly bamboo, and maple. Between the shrubs was a stone lantern, with a few stepping stones visible here and there. Apart from that, there were just weeds.

For the life of me, I could not see where those *chabana* could be. However, now and then, Sensei would slip on some geta clogs, pick up her floral scissors, and go to snip some from the shrubbery.

Displayed in the *tokonoma*, the flowers of delicate grasses and blossoms on otherwise-bare twigs struck a valiant note in spring, invoked coolness in summer, added a touch of opulence amid the dreariness in autumn, and stood out crisp and fresh in winter. Solomon's seal, bridal wreath, St. John's wort, fritillary, white egret flower, Japanese anemone, forked viburnum, spike winter hazel . . . We heard more names than we could count.

When it came to camellias—the queen of *chabana*—Sensei had at least thirty varieties in her garden, even counting only those that she had mentioned. Kochō-wabisuke, Kamo-honnami, Seiōbo, Sodekakushi . . . The list went on.

While I could not spot them out in the garden, no matter how hard I peered, there was no doubt that Sensei had been out there in her geta, scissors working. It was as though she had another, secret garden hidden away within the one I could see.

Camellias have to be in bud—you can't use them if they have already started to bloom. Even so, Sensei would choose a single plump bud that looked as though it would start to open up, petals parting slightly, during our lesson in the afternoon.

"It'd be better if this leaf was facing this way a bit more, wouldn't it? Come on, won't you turn a little further this way? Please?" For some reason, Sensei was cajoling the flower under her breath as she placed it in the vase.

"You probably think this is easy," she remarked.

"Yes."

It really did look simple.

"On the contrary. Arranging the flowers naturally, 'as they are in the field,' as we say in Tea, is very tricky, you know," said Sensei. "The simpler it looks, the more difficult it is."

Sometimes, Sensei would tell us not only what the flowers were called, but also the origins of those names.

One curious plant had a tiny pale green flower about the size of a sesame seed, right in the middle of the leaf. Sensei said, "The flower looks like it's on a raft, doesn't it?"

Glancing at it again, I saw what she meant. The little dot of a flower in the middle of the leaf really did seem like a blossom that had fallen from the riverbank onto a raft floating downstream.

"That's why it's called *hana-ikada*—floral raft," Sensei explained.

Indicating another plant with small white flowers on a long, slim, bifurcated spike, she told us, "The two parts bloom together, so they call it *futari-shizuka*—the two Shizukas. There's another variety of *Chloranthus* with only a single spike. That's called *hitori-shizuka*—Shizuka alone."

A row of plump, pink, heart-shaped flowers dangled from the long, slender stem of bleeding heart, whose Japanese name translates as "sea-bream-fishing-grass." The thin stem was bent, just like a fishing rod.

"Don't you think it looks just like a big catch of sea bream on a fishing rod?" asked Sensei.

People in days gone by named many flowers for the images conjured up by their shapes. My interest in *chabana* surged upon discovering this.

"Sensei, this one was goldfish grass, wasn't it?" I asked.

"No, not goldfish. Sea bream," she corrected.

"Oh, yes. Sea-bream-fishing-grass." I remembered now: "goldfish grass" was the common name for snapdragon.

Another day, I tried again. "Sensei, today's flower is . . . ummm . . . wintersweet, isn't it?"

"No, it's the same color, but that's not it. This is *mansaku*, Japanese witch-hazel. It's the first thing to bloom in early spring and they say that *mansaku* is a corruption of *mazu saku*—first-to-bloom."

Through exchanges like that, we learned the names of seasonal *chabana,* one or two at a time.

Scrolls

"When you enter a tea room, look at the scroll and flowers in the *tokonoma* first," Sensei instructed us. "The scroll is the greatest treat of all in Tea, you know," she added.

"Treat?" I echoed, bewildered.

The sweets and the tea I could happily call treats. Tea utensils were astonishing. The pretty little seasonal flowers and plump camellia buds were lovely, too.

The scrolls were the only thing that left me cold.

"Can you read today's scroll?" Sensei asked.

Whether because the calligraphy was so dexterous or just downright inept, I could not read a single character.

Sometimes the brush strokes looked limp and formless, sometimes aggressively harsh. Either way, I felt a sense of annoyance, because I could not help but think that the calligraphers had gone out of their way to make the characters illegible to the uninitiated.

When I heard that the calligraphy was the work of notable Zen priests, it seemed certain that they had deliberately made the characters hard to read, to assert their superiority over others.

Announcing "Today's scroll is . . . ," Sensei would always read the words on the scroll aloud to us.

One beautifully sunny Saturday in May, she read out *"Kunpū minami yori kitaru—*A fragrant breeze comes from the south."

On a summer's day, when we were covered in a light sheen of sweat, it was *"Seiryū kandan nashi—*The pure stream flows ceaselessly."

In late autumn, when the maple and persimmon trees in the garden were ablaze with crimson leaves, *"Sōyō manrin no hana—*The frost-tinted leaves fill the forest with flowers."

Even I knew that the characters on the scroll represented something to do with the season.

But I found nothing appealing or enjoyable that would justify the description "the greatest treat of all."

When Sensei read the scroll aloud, we all just nodded and said, "I see." We became a lot more animated once the sweets were served, the room filling with exclamations of wonder and delight.

At least we were honest.

Waterfall

It was a fiercely hot Saturday just after the rainy season. The temperature had been above thirty degrees since before noon. As we walked to our Tea lesson, the asphalt on the sidewalk reflected the sizzling heat back at us.

The instant we stepped into Sensei's entrance hall, the perspiration began to trickle down my back. Mopping my brow with a handkerchief, I placed my belongings in a small box in the anteroom as usual, put on a pair of white socks, and entered the tea room.

After making my greetings, I glanced at the *tokonoma*.

Hanging there was a scroll that must have been as tall as an average person.

At the top of this long piece of paper was the imposing shape of a single character, written in thick, vigorous strokes:

Waterfall

Below it, all the rest of the paper was blank.

Instead of ending with the customary upward flick, the final stroke cascaded on down through the empty space and came to a stop near the lower edge of the scroll. The force of the calligrapher's brushwork had left tiny spots of black ink spattered across the paper.

Wow!

For a moment, I could feel the spray on my face.

A cool gust of air rose up from the pool below.

My sweat-soaked back felt fresher.

Oh, it's lovely and cool.

Another, rather thick scale fell from my eyes.

So that's what she meant about the scroll!

All at once, my impression of scrolls as incomprehensibly difficult was swept away.

You aren't supposed to read the characters with your head. You just need to look at them, like a painting. Once I set aside my preconceptions, what I had thought to be difficult and the height of arrogance actually resembled a riddle.

The brush-written characters that had so irritated me turned out to be pictographs rendered by free-wheeling and playful minds. With flair and a single brush, someone had brought a waterfall to life on the alcove wall so realistically that I could feel its spray.

How marvelous!

Sensei looked at me as if to say, "You see?"

From that day on, I viewed the *tokonoma* with new eyes.

O and Snow

During a lesson in mid-October, I found myself staring at the scroll, mystified.

It was not a word, or even a character. Someone had just drawn a great big circle with their brush.

Sensei said, "Today's scroll is . . . can anyone tell me?"

Nobody spoke.

"Don't you see?" asked Sensei. "It's the moon-viewing festival tonight."

"Oh! It's the full moon!"

A Japanese anemone and a single tall stem of silver grass stood in a vase under the moon.

*

One Saturday in December, the sky was sullen and the weather forecast had warned of snow along the mountains. Sensei read that day's scroll aloud to us: *"Rōsetsu ten ni tsuranatte shiroshi."*

"What's *rō setsu*?" I asked, unable to figure out the part before "reaches white to the sky."

"Snow that falls in December," she replied.

Peering closely, I made out a pattern of pale spots sprinkled across the cloth backing.

Oh, it's snow!

Reflexively, I closed my eyes and imagined fluffy white flakes whirling and dancing as they fell from the sky.

Scrolls made the wind blow, spray fly, the moon rise, and snowflakes dance.

I knew that if I turned up to my Tea lesson, there was bound to be a moment when I would think, *I'm so glad I came after all!*

While we repeatedly practiced increasingly incomprehensible *o-temae,* we enjoyed *wagashi,* held the utensils, admired the flowers, and felt the wind or water blowing out from the scroll.

We engaged all five senses—sight, hearing, smell, touch, and taste—as well as our imagination. Every week, single-mindedly, we savored the season of now.

Eventually, something started to change . . .

CHAPTER 7

Connect to Nature with All Five Senses

A Chance Insight

Another Saturday, another lesson.

My "guest" had finished her tea and I was about to rinse out the bowl.

Submerging the *hishaku* into the depths of the bubbling kettle, I took a generous scoop and slowly, carefully withdrew the steaming ladle. Once it was positioned right over the tea bowl, I gently tilted it to let the hot water flow out. The mellifluous trickle was accompanied by a cloud of steam that enveloped the earthenware vessel.

After swirling the water around the bowl, I tipped it out into the *kensui* and announced, "I will bring the *o-temae* to a close," as I had been taught.

Then I took a scoop of cold water, with the same motion as before. I dipped the *hishaku* into the center of the *mizusashi*, withdrew it, and poured the ladleful of water into the tea bowl.

As the tinkling stream filled the bowl, I had a flash of insight. It sounded different!

The hot water had a mellow, burbling timbre.

The cold had a clear tone with a hard edge, like a diamond.

They had always sounded identical to me. I had thought they *were* identical. But suddenly, for no apparent reason, they were different.

And, from that day on, they always were.

June Rain

It was a wet day. Sensei's door was hard to slide open in the rainy season, as the humidity made the sills of the wooden house swell.

Inside, the sliding paper screens, so crisp in winter, were starting to sag.

"Hello!" we called out.

"Oh my, it was good of you to turn up in this rain," said Sensei.

Upon entering the tea room, we could hear the rain distinctly as it fell.

The big raindrops splattered so noisily onto the leaves of the paper-plant that it sounded like someone was pelting it with dried beans.

The steady *pitter-patter, pitter-patter* like fingertips drumming on a tent was the sound of the rain bouncing vigorously off the big, round leaves of the Japanese cornel and the foliage of the hydrangeas in full bloom. It felt like being in a tropical rainforest.

"Yes, that's the rainy season all right," Sensei murmured, to nobody in particular.

And then it struck me that this downpour sounded different from the rain in autumn. November rain had a desolate, melancholy air as it seeped into the earth. But why? Rain was rain, wasn't it?

Oh! It's because the leaves are dead . . . The sound of the rain in June is the sound of young leaves repelling the raindrops! Listening to the rain, you can hear how old the leaves are!

(Splatter-splash, splatter-splash)
(Pitter-patter, pitter-patter)

The Aesthetics of Sound

"Come on, hold it a bit higher when you pour."

Sensei would admonish us about the same failing whether the water was hot or cold: we were supposed to leave a gap about the depth of the ladle's cup between the *hishaku* and the kettle or bowl below.

Visual beauty was not the only reason for this, Sensei told us. "If you pour from that height, the water sounds better, doesn't it?" she explained.

It was true that the one-cup gap gave the sound a crystalline quality.

"You see? That's the aesthetics of sound," said Sensei.

In the garden outside the tea room was a washbasin made from a hollowed-out rock. On days when we had a Tea lesson, it would be filled with clean water that we used to purify our hands and mouths. Sensei would leave the faucet very slightly open, so that a fine rivulet of water continued to dribble out.

When we had only just started to learn Tea, I thought that she had just forgotten to shut it off. But when, at the height of summer, I heard her say, "It's hot today, so I'm letting a bit more water run into the washbasin," I realized that it was a kind of natural soundtrack.

The trickle from the faucet etched a perpetual flow of ripples onto the surface of the small pool in the rock.

Whenever I was immersed in my *o-temae*, that murmuring flow was always there in the background. The sound of the water had percolated through my body and mind without my knowing.

The Babbling Brook in the Underground Mall

One day, at Shinjuku Station, I was overcome with a splitting headache.

I had been walking around for hours amid the hustle and bustle after a poor night's sleep, and I was exhausted. The pain was intense. It felt as though someone was squeezing my head with a pair of pliers. I wanted to get away from the crowds and rest somewhere quiet as soon as I could.

I stepped woozily onto an escalator that took me down to the food hall in the basement. Making my way through the hubbub of staff and shoppers, I found a small café offering old-fashioned Japanese desserts, tucked away in a corner. I flung my bags aside, flopped into a seat just inside the café's entrance, and ordered a bowl of *mitsumame*: fruit, agar jelly and red *endōmame* peas. Then I hunched in my chair clutching my head, which seemed ready to burst.

The moment I did so, the din drifted away. I felt I had been drawn into a bubble of stillness. It was a pleasant sensation, like a mountain stream trickling into my head and easing the tension in my brain before anything snapped. The limpid water seemed to filter down behind my eyes, soothing my frazzled nerves and bringing them back to life. I felt so comfortable that I kept my eyes closed for a while, wishing I could stay like that forever.

*

I don't know how long I spent curled up. Five minutes, maybe ten. When I lifted my head again, the pain was gone. Relieved, I ate the dessert that had been put in front of me. I felt relaxed. In just a few minutes, I had completely recovered, as if by magic.

I only noticed the sound when I stood up to leave. Hearing the babble of running water, I turned around and spotted a washbasin. Not a hollowed-out stone like Sensei's, but a ceramic vase that someone had placed in the mop sink under the faucet to catch the fine stream of trickling water. That was the sound that had permeated through to my overwrought nerves, helping me to unwind and curing my splitting headache.

How wonderful!

I was amazed. The sound of running water had had a positively mystical effect.

As a child, I had read a Greek legend about an immortal warrior. He fell in battle many times, but recovered as soon as both his hands touched the earth. I suppose this was meant to signify nature's restorative effect on humans.

Just hearing the sound of water relaxes people and helps them forget their fatigue. I had found a connection to nature without even being aware of it.

"Thanks so much!" I said as I left the shop, revived.

Remembrance of Smells Past

Then there was the scent that caught my attention the moment I stepped into Sensei's entrance hall one day. It was a clean,

Topping up the mizusashi *with fresh water.*
On top of the tana *are a* hira-natsume *and* hishaku

Plate section pictures:
Katsuhiko Ushiro
Mitsuyoshi Hirano (Shinchosha Photography Department) / images with * marked

Stone washbasin

Using the chashaku *to scoop* matcha *into the tea bowl*

On the tatami to the right of the bowl is the chasen

Hisssss

Charcoal glowing in the ro

Hanging scroll:
Waterfall, *by Gensho Miyanishi*

Hanging scroll: Picture of Master
Bodhidharma, *by Ekyo Hayashi*

Japanese anemone in an inazuka *bamboo vase**

Natsume *with* maki-e *decoration:*
Spring Field and Autumn Field, *by Kinsa Kawabata V**

Usucha
A crescent should break through the cloud of foam . . .

Dry sweets: Sagano
(Early Autumn in Sagano)
(Tsuruya-Yoshinobu; Kyoto and Tokyo)*

Dry sweets: Yoshino Kaiko
(Yoshino Nostalgia), Hana-akari
(By the light of the Cherry Blossoms)
(Matsuya Honten; Nara and Tokyo)*

Ajisai *(Hydrangea)*
(Komaki; Kita-Kamakura, Kanagawa)*

Hatsu-gatsuo
(Minochū; Nagoya, Aichi)

Ochiba *(Fallen Leaf)*
(Sasama; Kanda, Tokyo)

Koborehagi *(Fallen Bush Clover)*
(Shiono; Akasaka, Tokyo)*

Yuzu Manjū
(Nagato; Nihonbashi, Tokyo)

Dry sweets: Koshi no Yuki
(Yamatoya; Nagaoka, Niigata)

The yohō-dana *during* koicha-temae *in* ro *season.*
The mizusashi *is placed on the lower tier, while a*
hira-natsume *is displayed on the upper tier.*
The tea bowl (left) and chaire *inside a brocade bag (right)*
are lined up on the tatami in front of the mizusashi.

somehow smooth smell that reminded me of far-off bonfires. As I walked down the corridor, the realization came to me out of the blue.

It's the scent of charcoal!

Although I had been surrounded by this smell every time I visited the house, and I had been coming for years now, I had never noticed it before. I had no idea that charcoal had its own scent.

A dormant olfactory nerve must have suddenly woken up.

One day, while purifying the *chasen*, I noticed a musty odor as I raised the wet prongs almost to my nose, and recalled the rainy season at an old house where I had once lived. I remembered the damp boards of the veranda when I had dashed out to retrieve the washing from the line before an imminent cloudburst.

Another day, as I was about to lift the *hishaku* from the kettle, I heard a passing breeze whisper through the garden, rustling the bamboo leaves with its soft caress. I felt a sudden pang of heart-ache. Exactly the same breeze had been blowing on the day when I had wept to the strains of music from a far-off festival.

Lifting the lid of the wide-mouthed summer *mizusashi* evoked the earthy smell of the parched garden after rain and a feeling of exuberance that spread through my chest in anticipation of the freedom of being on vacation.

When I held a thick winter tea bowl in both hands and swirled hot water around inside to warm it, I was taken back to the loneliness of my early years as a sickly child, when I spent much of my time in bed.

Rain, wind, and water: smells from long ago, mingled with my feelings from those days, appeared out of nowhere before vanishing again like smoke.

It was like myriad former versions of me were living within my current self.

Mapped out in Flowers

Around the time I started to notice these sounds and smells, I also began to spot *chabana*. Flowers for the tea room alcove could be found everywhere.

The three or four square kilometers where I spent much of my daily life were transformed once I had mapped out my neighborhood in terms of the *chabana* with which I had a nodding acquaintance. It gave me something by which to navigate both time and space, not entirely unlike a dog keeping track of rivals and potential mates by sniffing telegraph poles.

In spring, a few patches of Japanese fairy bells bloomed on a mound of earth outside the house opposite, each little white flower hanging down like a bell at a Buddhist temple. The grassy area behind the apartment complex was home to a clump of *futari-shizuka*. The sloping embankments visible through the train window were engulfed in a sea of light purple Chinese violet cress. A row of fringed irises lined the fence between our house and next door. Chinese spiranthes flowered on the fence beside the car park, while Japanese bindweed twined around the guard rail, its pale pink flowers opening up one after another.

Until then, I had thought flowers were something you bought from a florist, but those were just one small corner of a much wider and more colorful world.

There were always plenty of flowers lining the road we took to our Tea lesson. When their bloom started to fade, the leaves on trees and bushes took on rich hues instead. Once the leaves fell, bright red berries or tiny buds formed on the branches.

Sensei treated the autumn foliage just like the flowers of spring. "When the leaves look like this, we call them *teriha*— shining leaves."

Even twigs bare of anything but berries or buds could be displayed in a vase. They, too, were *chabana*.

How blinkered a view I had taken of what "flowers" really were.

There was no such thing as a season without *chabana*. There was no such thing as a boring time of year.

CHAPTER 8

Be Here, Now

In Limbo

Three years had passed since I had finished university slap bang in the middle of what was being called an "employment ice age" for female graduates. Thanks to an acquaintance's connections, I had managed to find part-time work as a reporter and writer for a weekly magazine while I waited for an opening at a publishing company.

I did not have a desk at the magazine, as I was not a staff member. But neither was I a guest. I stayed in that limbo for years. Some people even told me to my face that I was wasting my life spending so long in a casual position.

Whenever I met up with old classmates who had found permanent corporate jobs, they would talk of wanting to quit, complaining of horrible bosses and grueling or just boring work. To me, though, those seemed like the troubles of people who had already found their niche, somewhere in one of those huge office buildings in the heart of the metropolis.

A wedding and baby boom was already underway within my circle of friends. Some moved overseas for their husbands' work. Others were desperately trying to balance their own jobs with raising a family. Everyone had set sail across the ocean of life.

Tea student turnover intensified, too. Yumiko had quit after graduating from university and marrying a classmate, while Mrs. Tadokoro the policewoman had stopped coming to lessons because she was about to have a baby. We were joined by two young women whose husbands had been transferred to Yokohama with their jobs, but both were gone within a year or two, one due to pregnancy and the other because her husband was moved again. A woman's twenties were a time of great upheaval.

Michiko had been there with me from the beginning, but, two years after graduating and joining a trading company, even she resigned and went back home to the countryside, as her parents were anxious to start introducing her to prospective husbands.

While everyone else around me was racking up the milestones of adult life—first job, marriage, baby—I was still floundering, unable even to secure full-time employment. At home, my parents would badger me, day in, day out, arguing that if I was not going to get a proper job, I should at least let them get to work finding a serious marriage prospect for me.

At university, I had been determined to be independent and have a career for life, but I had ended up a nobody. Even my part-time job at the magazine could vanish at any time.

I felt as if I was the only one whose life had not yet really begun. The clock was ticking, but I could not even find the starting line. The ground beneath my feet seemed unsteady, as though I was going through life on roller skates. I was in the grip of a maddening urge to *do* something, like someone on a moving train so impatient to get to their destination that they cannot sit still any longer and jump off to run there instead.

I fretted about needing to get up and running too. I just didn't know which direction to go.

*

In those days of frustration, my Tea lessons alone were as sedate as ever. I learned how to handle increasingly formal utensils, starting my study of *karamono o-temae* after three years and *daitenmoku* after five.

In *karamono o-temae,* thick tea is stored in a small medicine jar of Chinese or Southeast Asian origin—*karamono* literally means "Tang things," referring to items from China. A king could scarcely be treated with greater care than that little pot. In *daitenmoku,* a Tenmoku tea bowl, iron-glazed with a narrow foot, is placed on a stand, or *dai,* so that it does not touch the tatami.

No way was I ever going to have the opportunity to make tea for real guests with such formal utensils.

What's the point of practicing something I'm never going to do in real life?

My inner reservations notwithstanding, Sensei was rigorous in her instruction.

"No, no, no. That's when your thumb goes over the *chaire.*"
and
"Wrong. It goes over, from the other side . . . Yes, like that. Try it again, please."

Even though I was never actually going to use this procedure, Sensei would not let even a single finger move incorrectly.

I was desperate to get my life moving. My exasperation would mount as each Saturday rolled around: *Ugh, Tea again.*

This was no time to spend a leisurely afternoon kneeling and whisking. I was impatient to move forward, and I felt that

Tea was holding up my progress. Sitting still for hours seemed a major waste of time while everyone else was getting further and further ahead.

I made one mistake after another as my attention lapsed. I mixed up the front and back of utensils and forgot to return to my kimono fold the silk *dashibukusa* cloth used by guests when drinking thick tea. I could not find the patience to wait for the last drops of water to fall naturally from the empty *hishaku*. As the ladle moved from *mizusashi* to kettle and back again, it dripped constantly, soaking the tatami.

"You've drifted off somewhere, haven't you?" Sensei remarked.

I looked at her quizzically, unsure what she was getting at.

"Oh, it's no good when you're young—no focus at all," she muttered, as though to herself. Then she looked at me and said, "You've got to be right *here*."

Uncomprehending, I remained silent.

"When you sit in front of the kettle, you have to *be* in front of the kettle."

Pour Your Heart into It

Sensei once said to us, "I don't mind if you make mistakes. But you mustn't be careless. You have to really pour your heart into each and every little movement."

I gave her a dubious look. How can you tell when you've poured your heart into something? It's an abstract concept, not like putting rice into a bowl, where you can look at it and say,

"Yup, there it is." But Sensei always taught us precisely how to pour our hearts into our *o-temae*.

For instance, she might say, "When you lift the tea bowl and the *usucha* container, you're supposed to lift them together, but try to make sure the tea container leaves the mat just a fraction of a second before the bowl."

or

"Ah, now, when you hold the *chashaku* like that, don't hold it parallel to the tatami. Lower the tip very slightly. That makes it look more elegant . . . No, that's too low . . . Yes, that's just right. Good."

or

"You 'whisk' *usucha*, but when it's *koicha*, we talk of 'kneading' it. When you knead thick tea, think of it like mixing mineral pigments to make paint. And listen to the tea. It will tell you how much you need to knead it."

They say that God is in the details. Tea was one big obsession over innumerable tiny details.

If you took pains over each one as your *o-temae* progressed, they would start to call attention to themselves: "Hey! This needs to be a fraction earlier." "Lower the tip of the *chashaku* a bit." "Knead, don't whisk." I felt aware of every movement of my body.

"Now, try kneading the *koicha* while listening to it," said Sensei.

I poured a little hot water onto the tea and gradually mixed it in with the bamboo whisk. The prongs felt slightly heavy, like feet stuck in mud.

Is this what she meant about mixing mineral pigments?

After four or five slow strokes of the whisk, the characteristic rich, grassy aroma of *koicha*-grade tea filled my nostrils.

Oh, the tea leaves have just woken up!

The fragrance exploded out of the tea bowl, as though triggered by a chemical reaction.

Each May, tea leaves are plucked and processed before being packed into earthenware tea jars, which are sealed to let the full-bodied flavor develop. About six months later, in November, the seals on the jars are broken and the leaves are ground into a fine, bright green powder using a stone mill.

That scent was a sign that contact with light and moisture had woken the tea leaves from their half-year slumber in the jar, I fancied.

I continued to knead. Then a moment came when the prongs of the *chasen* suddenly became lighter as I stirred. The *matcha* and the water were originally two separate substances, but now their molecules had bonded to become tea, I realized. The subtle changes in sensation transmitted through the *chasen* seemed to have given me an insight into the microscopic world.

I hear you. I'll give you a bit more hot water now.

I rested the *chasen* on the left-hand side of the bowl and topped up the hot water. After thinning out the viscous *matcha* a little with the additional water, I continued to work the two elements together with kneading strokes of the *chasen*.

The sensation of resistance from the bamboo prongs changed again, abruptly becoming heavier. A kind of stickiness emerged amid the smoothness. Somehow, the surface of the thick tea had taken on a glossy, inviting sheen, like honey.

I realized that I had completed the entire task in silence. Sitting in front of the kettle, I had devoted myself entirely and whole-heartedly to the sensation of kneading the *matcha*, to making this one bowl of tea.

Not long before, I had been so restless about spending my time at Tea that I had nearly rushed out of the room. Now my impatience had evaporated, without my even noticing.

I had not drifted off anywhere else. I was *here*. One hundred percent.

The Daruma Scroll

One Saturday lunchtime, the day before I was due to sit my umpteenth entrance exam for a publishing company job, I called Sensei.

"Sensei, I'm afraid I'll have to skip the lesson today."

She knew the reason.

"Your big exam is tomorrow, isn't it? That's fine. Best of luck." I was about to hang up the phone when Sensei added, "Oh, Noriko? If you want to take a tea break while you're studying, feel free to pop over."

But I could not concentrate at all that afternoon. At this late stage, what difference would a book of questions about current affairs or a transcription test make? I was even more restless than usual.

I had always thought, *If only I didn't have to go to Tea, I could do something more useful with my time,* but now that I had actually skipped my lesson, I found myself at a loss.

I might as well have gone to Tea.

Suddenly, Sensei's words came back to me: "If you want to take a tea break, pop over."

It was already late afternoon. The lesson might have finished by now. Without stopping to pick up my *kaishi* paper and sweet pick, I dashed round to Sensei's house.

"Helloooo! Sensei!"

Breathlessly opening the door to the entrance hall, I saw that the lesson had indeed already finished. The house was silent and not a single pair of shoes was left in the entrance hall.

"Oh, hello!"

Sensei's face appeared, not from the door to the tea room, but from the garden beside the house, where she had been watering the flowers.

"Am I too late?" I asked.

"Not at all," replied Sensei. "Come on in. I'll make some tea."

In the dimly lit tea room, now empty of students, the kettle was hissing and steaming. Had Sensei been waiting for me?

I entered the room as usual and looked up at the *tokonoma*.

Hanging there was a scroll that I had never seen before: a black ink painting of the bearded figure of Daruma, the monk also known as Bodhidharma who reputedly founded Zen Buddhism. He glowered at me with his big, round eyes.

Why had Sensei chosen this scroll today?

I looked at her face, searching for an answer.

"I was wondering what to put up today," she said, "and since you've got that important exam tomorrow, I decided that a glare from Daruma might do you good. Well, go on, eat your sweet, now."

A hot lump seemed to have formed in my throat, leaving me unable to reply. As my eyes swam with tears, clouding my vision, I hastily bowed while raising the sweet plate in gratitude.

Partly because of a long tradition of roly-poly toys bearing his likeness, Daruma is associated with the saying "Fall down seven times, get up eight." His image represents the ability to bounce back from adversity, and a change in fortune for the better. Perhaps, in this case, it also signified what you might call a kick in the pants.

The scroll in the *tokonoma* always reflects the season. But there are more seasons than just spring, summer, autumn, and winter. There are also the seasons of our lives.

That day, Sensei had been kind enough to put up a scroll coinciding with my personal moment of truth. As dusk fell and the shadows lengthened in the tea room, the kettle hissed and steamed.

CHAPTER 9

Give It Time and Let Nature Do the Rest

Heartbreak

My cousin Michiko married a doctor who owned a large hospital up in Japan's rural northeast. Takeda-sensei and I both attended the lavish wedding. After that, Michiko had a few children in quick succession and became wholly absorbed in her family.

As for me, I ended up remaining a freelancer writing small articles for the weeklies, and also started to pen special features for women's magazines. Before I knew it, five years had passed and the world around me was full of people doing similar work. The term "freelance writer" began to gain currency in Japan, and my earlier frustration about being the only one whose life had not yet begun gradually melted away.

When I was twenty-seven, I became engaged to a man I had been dating for several years. Our wedding was only two months away when I learned of his betrayal.

It came as a bolt from the blue. I sobbed my heart out on the station platform, oblivious to those around me. Even my fiancé's death could hardly have been a greater shock.

If I simply accepted what had happened and married him anyway, I could avoid rocking the boat for everyone around me or hurting my parents, who were eager to see their daughter married at long last. The start of my new life of wedded bliss, as people put it, was right before my eyes.

But once the seeds of distrust sprouted, everything began to veer off course. There was no way I could marry him now.

When I decided to break off the engagement, Dad looked gaunt and weary, while Mom just buried her head in her hands.

Day after day, I asked myself, *Was that really the right thing to do?* I would think it through and ultimately conclude that I had no other choice, only to be gripped by the same doubts again half an hour later. I must have repeated that mental conversation with myself hundreds of times.

My sense of loss was immense. Every day, the pain felt raw, as though someone was scraping a concrete block over my skin. I soon fell into a deep pit of despair. My body felt weighed down with sandbags and I could not muster the energy to climb back out. I would suddenly feel suffocated, and take desperate gasps of air until I caught my breath again. Mentally and physically, I felt like an empty husk.

At the end of 1983, the longest, hardest winter I had ever endured began. I knew I had to get back on my feet, but I was at a loss as to how. I just patiently waited for time to pass.

When spring comes, it'll get warmer. The sun will shine brighter. I might feel better then.

The Longest, Hardest Winter

With all the turmoil over my broken engagement, I stopped going to Tea lessons for a while. Sensei knew what had happened. When I returned to the tea room two months later, nobody asked me a thing.

Our group of Tea students had a rather curious relationship somewhat different from friendship. We did talk about our private lives, but we weren't exactly close. Each week, we would arrive at the tea room one by one, take turns to practice *o-temae*, drink tea, and chat about the utensils or the sweets in low-key exchanges: "You know, I don't think we've had this sweet before, have we?" "Uh-uh—Sensei served it to us last year, too."

When our lesson ended, we all tidied up the *mizuya* and left Sensei's house together. Each time we reached a road or station where one of us took a different route than the others, we would bid each other farewell with a brief "See you next week."

Everyone must have known my situation. But everything was just the same as usual. Having that kind of relationship helped me a lot.

In January, the Japanese witch-hazel in Sensei's garden blossomed. This was the flower whose name, Sensei had told me, was derived from the phrase "first to bloom."

"In the traditional calendar, today is *daikan*," said the television newscaster, "the most bitterly cold day of the year."

So we've reached rock bottom, I said to myself. *It'll start getting warmer now.*

Around the time of the *setsubun* festival in early February, I went to my Tea lesson and found in the *tokonoma* another unfamiliar scroll.

"Do you know what it says?" asked Sensei.

None of us replied.

"It means 'The wise can overcome any adversity,' but the characters can also be pronounced as *Fuku wa uchi*—'in with good fortune,'" she explained, chuckling at the seasonal pun.

Sensei had brought out a red-lacquered rice measure full of roasted soybeans, which are traditionally thrown on *setsubun* with cries of "Out with the demons! In with good fortune!" And when I took my final slurp of *usucha*, the goddess Otafuku's jolly face appeared at the bottom of the tea bowl. The black lacquer *natsume* was encircled with a design that bore the name "Spring field": violets, dandelions, lotuses, and horsetails rendered in powdered gold.

"*Setsubun* means the day dividing two seasons," Sensei told us. "Tomorrow is *risshun*, which means that we're heading into spring."

Japan's traditional calendar divides the year into twenty-four solar terms, based on the position of the sun. Some—like *risshun*, the beginning of spring—are simply named after their position within the four main seasons, while others have names that describe seasonal phenomena. *Daikan* means "Great Cold," and *usui* refers to the return of rain after the snow. *Setsubun* marks the boundary between the winter and spring, falling between the last day of *daikan* and the first of *risshun*.

I used to feel that the names were out of sync with the actual seasons for which they were named. For instance, when someone mentioned *risshu,* the first day of autumn, I would think, *Autumn? But it's still early August. We're right in the middle of summer!*

The traditional calendar had seemed no more than a relic of the past.

But now I came to think of those names as signposts. *Setsubun* and *risshun* cheered me up, reminding me that spring would soon be here. The calendar seemed a poignant symbol of all living creatures' longing for the return of spring.

I heard that the plum trees had bloomed in the spa resort of Atami. The first southerly gales of the year swept the country, bringing gusts of warm air that seemed to herald the season of new beginnings. However, the year's progress was not straightforward.

Just as we had cast off our sweaters and were rejoicing in a run of sunny weather, a cold snap would plunge us back into the depths of winter. I became despondent as spring appeared to retreat into the distance. Back and forth the seasons battled, over and over again.

My emotions mirrored the seasons. Time after time, just as I was trudging toward brighter days, the wind would change and knock me off my feet.

As the Girls' Day dolls and peach blossom of early March disappeared from view for another year, a tepid rain began to fall. Frogs started to crawl out of hibernation. The canola flowers bloomed. One evening, the lemony-sweet fragrance of winter daphne began to waft through the darkened streets.

And then the vernal equinox arrived.

I've made it this far. I'm going to be fine.

I put a potted plant I had been keeping in my room out on the veranda, where it would catch the spring sunshine all day long. A few days later, heavy snow fell across much of eastern Japan. Just when I had thought that winter was over at last, one snowfall had been enough to see off the plant on my veranda. I realized exactly how hard it was for living things to survive winter.

Our ancestors must have found their feelings mirrored by the seasons this way too, I thought, as they struggled to make it through winter. Counting off the mini-seasons—*setsubun, risshun, usui*—must have given them cheer, helping them to persevere through the hardest times of their lives despite the trials of winter's repeated, unwelcome encores.

Maybe that was why *chajin* took such pains to celebrate each and every seasonal festival and event.

For the first time in my life, I felt I understood the true essence of the seasons.

Flowers had never moved me as much as they did that spring. I was myself again. But it took another winter before laughter came freely and naturally to me.

In the summer just after I turned twenty-nine, I secretly fell in love.

When I was thirty, I wrote my first book. The day I received an advance copy of it, I showed it to the object of my affections.

"We need to celebrate," he said. "Let's go for a walk under the cherry blossoms by moonlight."

We strolled hand in hand along the banks of the palace moat at Chidorigafuchi, where the flowers—and the picnics beneath—had passed their peak. Each gust of wind stirred up a swirling blizzard of pale pink petals. I was so happy, I burst into peals of laughter as we were showered with blossoms. And each time I laughed, my tears fell like rain. I had not believed that days like this would return.

CHAPTER 10

Things Are Fine
as They Are

Hitomi

I was now in my thirties. Work had suddenly become busy and my life was an endless round of interviewing people and writing articles in the shadow of looming deadlines.

I had to miss my Tea lesson more often than before, but, when I did go, tasty sweets and a bowl of hot tea were waiting for me in the same room filled with the scent of charcoal and the sound of water trickling into the stone basin outside.

Three other students attended the Saturday afternoon lesson in those days: Sanae, who was now working as a so-called "Office Lady"; a university student whose family name was Fukuzawa; and Yukino, another woman in her thirties, who was related to Sensei. I had been there longer than anyone else, but even the newest member of the group, Miss Fukuzawa, had been taking lessons for three years.

It was in my tenth year of studying Tea that we were joined by a fifteen-year-old newcomer. She turned up at the lesson in her school uniform, on her way home from Saturday morning classes. Below a pale forehead framed with fine baby hairs, her peachy, unblemished cheeks were tinged pink with nervousness.

"I'm looking forward to studying with you all," she said, with a small bow of the head that made her ponytail bounce.

Her name was Hitomi, and she looked like the heroine of a manga for teenage girls. Her petite build made her appear even younger than her years. Stars seemed to twinkle in her bright chestnut eyes.

"I've longed to study Tea ever since I saw it on TV," she told us, eyes agleam. "I was determined to start learning once I got to high school." I was surprised that Tea culture would hold any appeal for a girl of fifteen in this day and age.

Asked by Sensei to teach Hitomi how to fold her *fukusa,* Sanae readily complied, instructing the new recruit in great detail. "I'll have to be careful now," she joked. "It would be terrible if I taught Hitomi any bad habits!"

Our artless teenage novice became a kind of mascot for the class.

Hitomi learned it all from scratch just as I had, starting with how to open and close the door and how to walk across the tatami. In her nervousness, she swung her arms forward along with her legs as she tried to cross the tatami in six steps. We laughed uproariously and her face reddened like a tomato. Her bow was stiff and robotic. After her first *o-temae,* evidently sensing what a long road lay ahead, she gulped back tears and said, "I wonder if I'll ever be able to do it smoothly." We laughed. She squirmed and said, "I can't move—my feet have gone numb!" We laughed again.

She marveled at every little thing in the tea room.

"Wow! I've never seen such a beautiful tea bowl!"

and

"I've never had sweets like this before!"

and

"Oh, what a lovely *mizusashi*!"

And the stars twinkled in her big, round eyes.

We talk of people soaking things up like a sponge, and that was exactly how Hitomi learned, steadily absorbing everything that she was taught. There was something within her beyond obedience. She listened to Sensei's admonishments with a painfully serious expression and would watch intently as everyone else performed their *o-temae*, even after she had completed her own. If she spotted an elegant movement, she would lean forward, eyes sparkling, and ask, "Could you just show me that again?" Then she would practice the action herself.

Looking at Hitomi engrossed in her *o-temae*, Sensei murmured softly, "Watching her reminds me of the saying 'People become best at what they love the most.'"

Innate Talent

Hitomi's earnest, awkward *o-temae* rapidly became more polished.

One day, Sensei said, "Hitomi, I'd like you to whisk a bowl of *usucha* for each of us."

Hitomi acknowledged her request with a "*Hai*," and disappeared to the *mizuya*. Soon the door slid open and she reappeared with tea bowl and *natsume* in hand. Starting her *o-temae* as usual, she set the *hishaku* down on the *futaoki* with a *pock!*, then placed both hands on the tatami in front of her and bowed.

I was startled. Her profile was somehow sharper, as though a thin veil had been stripped away. Once stiff and angular, her shoulders and arms now had a more natural, rounded line that sloped gently down to her hands. Her supple motion as she lowered her head burned an afterimage into my eyes.

My gaze was inexorably drawn toward her movements. Her slim, careful fingers gave her gestures a delicate expressiveness as she rotated and lifted the *chasen*. She was not simply performing a prescribed series of actions; rather, the movements seemed to flow as naturally as the blood through her veins. Gently enfolding the tea bowl in both hands as if to warm and protect the life force within, she swirled the hot water around inside it with unhurried grace. Her posture was beautifully straight. This high school student had the confident features of an adult woman.

Nobody uttered a word. The boiling kettle hissed. The atmosphere was intense as we sat there, captivated.

I wish I could stay like this forever, I thought.

I had the feeling that everyone else was thinking the same thing.

So that's what they call innate talent.

Anyone can sing karaoke. But few can inspire goosebumps and move you to tears with their performance. The same goes for cooking. Anyone can cook something that will fill the belly, but not many people can make a meal so good that it warms the heart as well.

Hitomi swished the *chasen* back and forth with a sound like a rushing brook, then slowly, gently drew the spiral of the hiragana character *no* and lifted the whisk from the bowl. I accepted the steaming bowl, placed it before my knees, and bowed. "Thank you for the tea you have prepared," I said, reciting the customary phrase, then raised the bowl to eye level as a gesture of gratitude to the tea.

A deep green crescent broke through the cloud of foam covering the jade liquid. I turned the tea bowl. A verdant aroma rose up with the steam, passing through my nostrils to light up my mind like the sun's rays. I drank the hot *usucha* in three sips, draining the bowl with a gentle slurp. Lingering on my tongue, the aftertaste was first sweet, then slightly bitter, and finally refreshing.

I don't think Hitomi realized that she had a talent for Tea. However, whether or not they know it, people who are immersed in an activity that demonstrates their talents affect everyone around them.

Just like a runner in a marathon breaking away from the pack to streak ahead, Sanae's *o-temae* suddenly became remarkably beautiful. Each gesture of her hands conveyed a sense of freshness. The tension in her shoulders evaporated and they took on a more womanly slope. You could see she was comfortable trusting her hands to move naturally rather than thinking with her head.

Eventually, another one broke away from our pack. This time it was Miss Fukuzawa, the university student. Where once she had looked lethargic as she walked across the tatami, now she radiated alertness all the way to her fingertips. The *hishaku* traced a beautiful arc through space as she scooped hot water from the kettle.

Everyone had suddenly grown up.

No Confidence

Inspired by the other students' stunning metamorphoses, I took greater care over my own *o-temae*, paying attention to each movement. But, as ever, I had no idea what I was really doing.

If Sensei said, "I'd like you to do *sumi-temae*, Miss Morishita," I would reply, "*Hai*," and lay and replenish the charcoal as I had learned.

If instructed to do *koicha o-temae,* I would reply, "*Hai*," and perform the procedure for making thick tea.

If told, "Ah, now, you should do that with your left hand, not your right," I would reply, "Oh, sorry," and correct my mistake immediately.

And then the moment was gone.

But what was *sumi-temae*? What were *koicha-temae* and *usucha-temae*? I was practicing the procedures, but I did not understand what they *were*. And I could not put my finger on just what it was that I did not understand.

It was like having all the interior decor for the rooms of a house without the structure of the building itself. The color of the wallpaper, the lamps, and the curtains had been chosen. However, there was not a trace of any of the house's structural elements: no foundations, no pillars, no walls, no connecting hallways— nothing. The furnishings were just floating around in a void.

It was no good saying to me "You know, if you put the door to the living room here, it blocks off the kitchen," or "Oh, no! How do we get into the bedroom?" It meant nothing to me.

I had not thought about how the rooms were linked to one another. I did not even know that what I was building was a house . . .

That was why, although I had studied Tea for more than a decade and was learning advanced procedures like *karamono* and *daitenmoku*, there were still so many utterly elementary things that I just didn't know. I made the same mistakes, time and again. Sensei even sighed and said, "When I was studying Tea as a young woman, one of my teacher's other students would never give Sensei a reason to correct her a second time—once was enough. You need to start taking it as seriously as she did."

But I still gave her cause to scold me for the same thing over and over, until she could take it no more and exclaimed her pet phrases: "It's like everything I teach you just rolls right off! I'm too cross for words!"

Of course, I was not the only one who had this problem. Everyone made mistakes and was scolded, week in, week out. But we all just lowered our gaze, apologized, and carried on regardless.

My Complex

Gradually, though, I stopped finding it funny.

Thirteen years had passed since I had started to learn Tea. I would soon reach *bonten* level. In our tradition of Tea, the most advanced *o-temae* performed by men is *shin-no-daisu*, in which utensils are displayed on a large, black-lacquered formal utensil stand called a *daisu*. For women, the highest-level *o-temae* is *bonten*, a procedure that involves handling a particularly valuable *chaire* of Chinese origin, which is placed on a small tray.

Hitomi and Fukuzawa, at least, saw me as a veteran *chajin*.

"Miss Morishita, we only need a bamboo *futaoki* today, don't we?"

"I think that's fine, but . . ." I replied, tailing off uncertainly.

Then Hitomi, my junior in both age and experience, piped up beside me with the right answer: "The *futaoki* is going to be displayed on a *tana* today, so shouldn't it be ceramic?"

Despondent, I dropped my gaze to the *mizuya* floor. Every time someone asked me something, I felt compelled to cover up my lack of confidence.

Although I had attended many *chakai*, I was always petrified when I had to help out at one. Unlike at a lesson, I could not consult Sensei about every little thing. My heart was in my mouth whenever my turn came to perform *o-temae*. Because they were large public gatherings, I was conscious that I must not put a foot wrong, but the more I dwelled on this, the more nervous I became, and I would end up making one unbelievably rudimentary error after another.

They say that you can tell someone's character from their split-second responses. I knew that mine were no help at all, so I would quake in my *tabi* each time someone asked me a question.

Perhaps I just wasn't cut out for Tea.

If I am honest, the thought had occurred to me before. Tea was a world of countless rules, but there were times when adaptability and quick-wittedness were indispensable. You needed to be able to read the situation, waiting an extra second or so for someone else to make a move, or deciding instantly which of the two things you had to do took precedence, or moving something out of the way before it became an obstacle later. These spur-of-the-moment improvisations outside the rules give people the chance to show off their proficiency.

However, that was my principal failing. I had been conscientious to a fault since childhood, doing my level best to follow all the rules. I lacked the composure to look at the broader picture or the flexibility to play things by ear. My outlook was as blinkered as a cart horse, trotting along a straight path without even glancing to either side. I thought only of what I was doing, and, after some three decades, that maladroitness had become part of my character.

Hearing people describe consideration for others as something that came naturally rather than having to be learned, I felt as though I lacked a component that everyone else had, as if my appendix were missing.

I took it seriously, regarding it as a deficiency on my part. It was something of a complex of mine. I was so helpless in the face of my over-conscientiousness that I even gave my all to being depressed.

I envied considerate people.

The one who demonstrated her leadership at *chakai* was Yukino. We relied on her completely, referring to her affectionately as our big sister. This was not because she was the oldest of the Saturday students, but rather because she was so good at stepping up and taking charge when the need arose.

Under her direction, duties such as marshaling the guests, neatly lining up their *zori*, washing up, whisking tea in the *mizuya*, and serving sweets and tea were shared out between all of us, from older ladies in their sixties down to Hitomi in her teens. We all adapted to our circumstances as we carried out our allotted tasks.

Everyone apart from me seemed to have more than enough consideration for others. Most people studying Tea were probably like that in the first place. I gradually started to feel out of place.

Because of my conscientious nature, being scolded when I was feeling down would hit me like a slap in the face. One day, Sensei chided me about the way I held the ladle: "When you grip the *hishaku*, your hand looks like a big, knuckly fist. Can't you hold it a bit more delicately? You've been learning Tea for more than ten years—you should start figuring out ways to refine these things."

Although she had told me before that I needed to find a more elegant way to hold the *hishaku*, the criticism struck me in a particularly sensitive spot that day. As I stared down at the hand that Sensei had complained about, I could not stop my eyes filling with tears. I just wanted to get out of there and go home.

A Decision after Thirteen Years

I was in low spirits for a few days after that.

I'm still getting it wrong after all this time. I'm not confident and I'm not considerate, either. And my hands are knuckly too . . . I'm just not cut out for Tea.

It was not as though the lessons had been my idea in the first place. I had simply begun going so that Michiko and I could stop off somewhere for a chat on our way home. But Michiko had long since departed to get married. So many girls and women had joined our group, only to leave again because of marriage, babies, or their husband's job. Left behind, at some point I had become an old-timer.

When I began studying Tea, Sensei often used to tell us, "There's an old saying: three days, three months, three years. In other words, if you stick with something past the three-year mark, you'll keep going with it in the long run."

I was well past three years—counting back, I was already in my thirteenth year of studying Tea. Why had I not given up already?

I was the first-born child and had been brought up to be a good, hardworking girl. It seemed to me that I had struggled on because I was helpless to break free from my parents' warnings not to give up halfway once I had started something. I had even thought it would be unfair to Sensei, who had persevered in teaching me properly without ever letting things slide.

On the plus side, waiting for me when I went to my lesson were tea and seasonal *wagashi* and gorgeous utensils, and I would always have that moment where I thought, *I'm so glad I came after all!*

That was the nebulous reason why I carried on. But as our lessons went into greater depth, I realized that I was not actually cut out for Tea. When I saw people taking to it like a duck to water, it became even clearer that I was no duck.

Evidently my place in the world was not to be found here, either.

I've spent thirteen years of my life on something I'm not even suited to. What an idiot!

I laughed ruefully at myself.

I'm going to quit Tea.

The decision made itself as the autumn of 1989 drew to a close. Maybe I would feel something was missing at first, once I had lost the place I had been going to for so many years. But that was bound to pass quickly, and I would be able to spend my Saturday afternoons more enjoyably. One day, I would talk of Tea in the past tense, saying, "Oh yes, I used to study that years ago."

Once I had made my mind up, I felt a twinge of loneliness. But that loneliness was very similar to relief.

Chaji

I had made up my mind to quit at the end of the year, but I continued going to my last few lessons without confiding in Sensei about my decision.

Then, one day, Sensei announced, "We're going to practice holding a *chaji*."

*

Most people probably think a *chaji* is the same as a *chakai*. But they are actually completely different things. I had discovered that when Michiko was still coming to lessons with me.

Sensei had told us that she was taking us to learn about *chaji*, and I had thought that we were just going to another tea gathering. However, we stopped at an outwardly unremarkable house in a quiet residential street. Calling out a hello to announce our arrival, we stepped inside.

Behind the doors of that ordinary house was a tea room for hire. The snug little room was surrounded by a peaceful garden. We were the only guests. Tucked away from the world like this, the atmosphere was somehow different.

What astonished me was the peculiarly small entrance. The doorway was positively Lilliputian. You could not get through unless you crouched down and lowered your head. Following Sensei, one after the other, Michiko and I curled ourselves up like moles and bowed as we crawled inside.

The dimly lit tea room was just four and a half mats in size, barely more than seven square metres. There was something clandestine about it that I found a little exciting.

The host—whom I took to be the lady of the house—entered and performed *sumi-temae*. Then, for some reason, we were each brought a tray of food.

Huh? Is this a restaurant?

Side by side at the front of each tray stood two black-lacquered lidded bowls.

Following Sensei's lead, we took the lids off both bowls simultaneously, one in each hand. Clouds of steam rose up and the seashore aroma of dashi stock tickled my nose. The bowl on the right contained a small puddle of soup and a single piece of something I didn't immediately recognize. The bowl on the left held no more than two mouthfuls of white rice.

Is this all?

However, when we took a sip, Michiko and I spontaneously turned to look at each other, eyes sparkling. The sharp scent of yuzu cut through the rich, complex flavors of dashi and white miso. The mysterious chunk turned out to be a piece of soft wheat gluten from which stock gradually oozed as we chewed. There might not have been much rice, but each shining grain was sweet and tasty.

"Don't eat all your rice—you need to leave a mouthful," said Sensei, but it was already too late.

"Sorry, it was just so good," I said guiltily.

When I reached with my chopsticks for the sea bream sashimi beyond the bowls, Sensei stopped me: "Not yet. You don't touch the dish on the other side until the saké has been served."

"Really? There's saké, too?" I asked, amazed.

The saké arrived chilled. A small trickle was poured from a beautiful glass flask with a long spout like a bird's beak into my shallow, red-lacquered cup, and I took a sip. The liquid felt rich and velvety on my tongue. It was lovely.

The rest of the meal was even more astounding. We were treated to a veritable banquet. One after another the dishes came: simmered vegetables, grilled fish, slow-cooked delicacies, vinegared salad, and a selection of other savory treats to complement the saké . . . There were generous refills of soup, and extra helpings of rice were served from a large wooden tub. Everything was delicately flavored and beautifully arranged on exquisite tableware. The gold *maki-e* patterns on the black lacquer dish for the simmered vegetables gleamed mysteriously in the half light. Many cups of saké were shared that afternoon.

Our leisurely, elegant meal seemed to go on forever.

This is just like one of those long Italian lunches! I thought, recalling how people in Italy would spend three hours at the dining table. They would eat their fill of antipasti, followed by mountains of pasta, salad, and huge servings of meat, washed down with a large bottle of Chianti, even at lunchtime. Dessert would be followed by a *digestivo* of some kind.

I was utterly content.

It was about two and a half hours later when the meal finally ended and we stood up. I had completely forgotten why we were there and thought that it was time to go home.

However, Sensei said, "Right—now we go out to the garden and wait for the host to make the preparations."

"Preparations?" I asked.

"It's time for tea," she replied.

Oh, of course! This is a Tea lesson.

"The meal we've just had is called *kaiseki*," Sensei continued.

"You eat it to line the stomach before drinking the tea, so that you can fully appreciate the flavor of the *matcha*."

That endless, luxurious meal had just been the warm-up!

A *chaji* is a mammoth undertaking. We went outside and stretched our legs, then sat on the bench and gazed at the impeccably manicured garden while we waited for the second half to start. It was something like the intermission between the acts of a play.

And then we crawled back in through that little doorway to find a shaft of light now shining through the dimness of the tea room. The bamboo screens that had covered the windows until shortly before had all been rolled up.

The *koicha-temae* began amid an air of great solemnity.

It was early evening by the time the *chaji* ended, several hours after our lunchtime arrival. Enjoying a single bowl of tea had taken up half a day.

The cuisine, the tableware, even the layout of the food— everything had been prepared with fastidious care. The mood had mellowed as we shared several cups of saké, and then we took a short break in the water-sprinkled garden before returning to find the bamboo screens rolled up, transforming the lighting of the tea room. All this, just for a bowl of *matcha*.

I never knew such luxury existed . . .

But, despite this experience, I had never before made the connection between my weekly Tea lesson and *chaji*. I had thought of those few hours of indulgence beyond that narrow doorway as

129

some kind of special occasion, so when Sensei announced that we were going to practice holding a *chaji* it did not click with me right away what that meant.

"I'll prepare everything for the *kaiseki* meal, with the help of my friends," Sensei told us. "We're going to do this properly, the formal way, so you'll need to study some books about how a *chaji* is done."

Sensei was really fired up. She had already decided on the seating order.

"As it's an important role, I'd like Yukino to be main guest."

"Yes, Sensei."

"Second guest will be Miss Fukuzawa. Third guest, Hitomi."

Each signaled her acknowledgement in turn.

"The last guest also has lots to do, so I'm relying on you, Sanae."

"Yes, Sensei."

And then she said, "Miss Morishita, you'll be the host."

Sensei knew nothing of my plans to quit. I dithered about what to do for a brief second, but then replied, "Yes, Sensei. I'll give it a try."

"At the risk of repeating myself, it's your responsibility to read up on your roles beforehand," Sensei told us. "The host and main guest in particular need to have a good grasp of the *chaji*'s overall flow, or you won't know what you have to do. So make sure you study hard."

I realized why Sensei had emphasized this point when I opened a book about Tea procedure to the *chaji* section.

What have I gotten myself into?!

Skimming the chapter left me even more confused than before. I went back through the text several times, but it was way over my head. Realizing that I needed to get serious, I armed myself with my red pencil and stared at the page. The book stared back. The full picture still eluded me. I drew up a kind of script, which covered no less than six closely handwritten pages. The magnitude of the undertaking hit me again.

Many of the set phrases sounded straight out of a period drama: "Allow me to serve you the humble repast that I have taken the liberty of preparing from what I had in the kitchen." "Would you be so good as to lend me your saké cup for a while?" Words on a page were not enough to give me a feel for it all, so I tried doing a run-through with small dishes from the kitchen at home.

Ironically, it was only once I had made up my mind to quit that I started studying Tea in earnest. I rehearsed over and over again. Eventually, from the mists of obscurity, the vague outlines of a *chaji* began to form in my head.

On the big day, Sensei's kitchen looked like it belonged in a traditional inn, piled to overflowing with bowls and dishes. She and her helpers had been hard at work preparing the food since the day before. The scroll in the *tokonoma* read:

> *Matsu ni kokon no iro nashi*
> Young or old, the pine is always green

She had chosen this scroll for our very first *chaji* because of the pine's symbolic associations with starting a new chapter in life.

I was wearing a pink unpatterned kimono with a single crest that I had borrowed from my mother. As the time of the guests' arrival approached, I sprinkled water on the garden and the floor of the entrance hall, to symbolize the freshness of dew and show our guests that everything was ready. They arrived and entered the tea room just before noon.

"Now, go and make your opening greetings," Sensei said.

"*Hai.*"

I slid the door open and we all bowed as one.

And so our *chaji* began.

A Reason for Everything

Once, in elementary school, I sprinkled some iron filings on a piece of card and moved a magnet around underneath. Like soldiers obeying orders, the scattered particles instantly formed neat ridges along the lines of force, following the magnet as it moved.

The various *o-temae* that I had learned over the years were dispersed across the corners of my mind. But, thanks to my experience of hosting that *chaji*, everything had fallen into line as neatly as those iron filings, flowing from *sumi-temae* to *kaiseki* to *koicha-temae* to *usucha-temae*.

One by one, the jumbled pieces of the jigsaw had come together. Now I could see the reason for that sequence:

Koicha is high in caffeine. As the thick tea is too strong to drink on an empty stomach, *kaiseki* is eaten beforehand to fill the belly. After the meal comes dessert, in the form of *wagashi.*

. . . I see! At our lessons, we're leaving out the kaiseki *part of the* chaji *and just practicing the* wagashi *and* koicha *elements . . .*

A tasty bowl of *koicha* needs hot water, but once the weather turns chilly in November, the water is very cold at first and takes time to boil.

. . . That's why we do sumi-temae *before the meal in winter!*

In *ro* season, the guests huddle around the sunken hearth while the charcoal is being laid.

. . . Looking at the glowing charcoal helps the guests to keep warm! Then the water boils while they eat their meal, heating the cold room. Of course—how clever!

Once I understood that, I realized how efficient the process actually was. So many things fell into place. There was a reason for everything. Nothing was wasted.

The *chaji* was the culmination of everything that we had been learning at our weekly lessons. We had practiced the procedures over and over again every Saturday, starting with *usucha* and then moving on to *koicha* and *sumi-temae.* All of it had been rehearsal for a *chaji,* broken down into its component parts.

We were like orchestra sections—violins, cellos, flutes, horns—who had separately practiced individual movements for years and years. Today, we had performed all the movements from start to finish as a full orchestra for the first time—faltering and halting as that performance may have been . . .

Dusk had fallen by the time we left Sensei's house. Walking to the crossroads where we usually said goodbye, we were all ruminating on the same thing. We had been on stage together. And we had found ourselves performing a magnificent symphony.

Turning Point

The following week, our lessons returned to normal. It was a fine Saturday in late November.

The sky was cloudless and blue, the air cold and clear. I opened our front gate to find the road covered in fallen leaves, without an inch of asphalt to be seen. They crunched like cornflakes underfoot as I walked to Sensei's house. The trees lining the roadside were bare, transforming the townscape.

Huh? Where am I?

For a split second, I had the illusion that I had wandered into an unfamiliar neighborhood. It was like the feeling you get when snow blankets the ground, but this time the town was buried under fallen leaves.

When I arrived at Sensei's house and slid open the tea room door, it was warm and cozy inside.

"Come in," said Sensei. "Yukino was just about to start making *koicha*."

Crossing the room to take my seat, I glanced at the *tokonoma* as usual.

The scroll read:

Mon wo hirakeba ochiba ōshi
When I opened the gate, fallen leaves lay in drifts

I felt as though it was speaking to me: "Don't you think so? After all, you've just walked here through that very scene!"

"Well, go on, hurry up and take your sweet," Sensei urged. "I popped up to Sasama in Kanda to get it this morning."

Opening the lid of the black lacquer sweet box in front of me, I let out an involuntary cry of delight. Standing out against the darkness within was a curled-up fallen leaf, its color gradually shading from yellow to blazing orange.

After admiring the sheer beauty of the confection's subtle gradation of hue, I cut it into a few pieces with my sweet pick and took a bite. The leaf, crafted from white bean paste, was wrapped around a small ball of pureed azuki beans. It was exquisitely smooth and sweet.

Kneeling in front of the kettle as steam billowed out, Yukino kneaded the *koicha*. She gave the *chasen* a final swirl and gently lifted it from the bowl. Fat droplets of dark green tea rolled lazily down the bamboo prongs. Fingers neatly aligned, her hand turned the tea bowl twice to face me and then reached out to put it in the customary spot along with the *dashibukusa*.

"Excuse me for drinking before you."

I bowed to the guest on my left, took the solid Oribe ware tea bowl in my hands, and brought it to my lips.

The hot, thick green liquid mingled with the sweetness of the *wagashi*. A well-kneaded bowl of *koicha* makes me feel as though I am losing myself in layers of rich, deep flavor, like eating crab tomalley or foie gras. I had reflexively grimaced at the bitterness the first time I drank it, but a part of me had come to relish that viscous texture without realizing it. My sense of taste seemed particularly clear that day, as though each of my taste buds had blossomed.

When I lifted my face from the tea bowl, I felt as if a verdant breeze had whistled between the very cells of my body. The refreshing aftertaste left even my saliva tasting rich and sweet.

I'm so happy right now.

Yukino cleansed the utensils to finish the *o-temae,* then rose and opened the sliding paper door. And as she did, I saw through the glass door across the hallway a bottomless blue sky. It almost seemed it might sweep me up far, far above the ground.

Oh, this feels so good!

Looking toward the heavens, I let out a deep breath and freed my mind.

Just then, I heard a voice inside my head say, "Things are fine as they are, right?"

Huh?

"You can quit whenever you like. In the meantime, just come and enjoy the tea. That's what you've been doing until now, after all. Things are fine as they are."

Although the words came from somewhere within me, they seemed to float down from the sky.

It was not a question of deciding whether to quit or not. It didn't have to be yes or no. Until I actually quit, I was still in a state of not-having quit, and that was fine.

That's right. It doesn't matter that I'm not considerate by nature. It's okay for me to be more experienced, but still undependable. I won't compare myself to anyone else. All I need is to keep going along the Way of Tea at my own pace.

I unburdened myself of the load I had been carrying. The tension left my shoulders and I felt suddenly lighter. I was completely present.

Why didn't I realize this before? Things are fine as they are!

CHAPTER 11

Parting Is Inevitable

Delayed Independence

When I was thirty-three, I belatedly flew the nest and began living alone about thirty minutes by train from my former home. Where it had once taken me less than ten minutes to walk to my Tea lesson, I now had to take the train, and it became my habit to visit my parents on my way home on Saturdays.

Whenever I showed my face at their house, my father would say, "Oh, you're here, are you? Have dinner with us. We should eat together from time to time." All through the meal, he would wear a contented smile, happily drinking saké and insisting that I join him. At sixty-six, his hair was snow-white, and he had started to look like the epitome of a kindly old man.

"It's already late, so you'll have to stay the night," he would say, even though it was not yet eight o'clock. Sometimes, he did not even wait for darkness to fall before remarking on the lateness of the hour. "It's already late" became his pet phrase.

But I never once took up the invitation. No matter how late it was, I always returned to my own apartment, as though turning my back on his eagerness to be together as a family. Ever since my early teens, I had been the daughter who rebelled against her father— and with the brattish obstinacy of independence too long delayed.

Ichi-go Ichi-e

Takeda-sensei had recently started arranging the occasional *chaji* practice for us, setting aside days separate from our ordinary lessons. We all took turns playing the part of host and guests.

When I had been through a full *chaji* a few times, I realized that it had much in common with the dinner parties I had seen in foreign films. Guests at a *chaji* receive a written invitation and attend in formal attire, gathering in a waiting room called the *yoritsuki*. Once all the guests are assembled, they enter the tea room, which is effectively the dining room. At a grand dinner party, when the long meal has drawn to a close, the ladies withdraw to touch up their makeup while the gentlemen go off to smoke cigars. At a *chaji*, too, a tobacco tray with a long, slender bamboo pipe and other smoking paraphernalia is always placed on the garden bench where guests take a break after the *kaiseki* meal.

Japanese people are now familiar with the ritual of tasting wine at a restaurant, in which a little is poured into a glass for them to inspect the color and check the bouquet and flavor before pronouncing it acceptable. There is a similar exchange between the host and main guest at a *chaji* after the first sip of *koicha*. The host asks, "Is the tea to your liking?" and the guest replies, "Yes, it is excellent." There follows an exchange between guest and host like a sommelier introducing a 1983 Chateau Margaux:

"What is the name of the tea?"

"It is Wakamatsu-no-mukashi."

"Where is it from?"

"It is from Ippodo."

Tea and wine had a lot in common.

Tea leaves plucked in May are packed into earthenware jars and stored until autumn. In early November, when the *ro* is opened, the most formal *chaji* of all takes place: the *Kuchikiri-no-chaji*. The seal on the jar is broken, the leaves are ground into powder with a stone mill, and tea is made from them for the first time. That day marks the beginning of drinking that year's tea. This is why *robiraki* is described as "New Year for *chajin*." All this is reminiscent of Beaujolais Nouveau Day, also in November, when the first of the new wine produced that year is uncorked.

When we held a *chaji*, Sensei would often say, "Make sure you take it seriously, everyone. A *chaji* is a once-in-a-lifetime experience for both host and guests, so you have to pour your heart into it."

The phrase Sensei used was "*ichi-go ichi-e*," which literally means "one time, one meeting."

"Even if the same host holds a *chaji* with the same guests many times, each gathering is a unique occasion that will never be repeated, just like today will never come again," Sensei told us. "That's why you must approach a *chaji* in the spirit of *ichi-go ichi-e*."

Sensei's words did not quite hit home for me. I understood the part about it not being the same occasion even if exactly the same people were present. But why did we have to get hung up on a *chaji* being a "once-in-a-lifetime encounter" when it was just people getting together to eat a meal and drink tea?

Strolling home from our *chaji*, I asked Yukino, "Don't you think it's a bit over the top?"

"It's probably something to do with the olden days, when Rikyū was alive," she replied.

When Sen no Rikyū codified Tea in the sixteenth century, as Japan's turbulent Sengoku period was drawing to a close, the warlords Oda Nobunaga and Toyotomi Hideyoshi were in power.

"A friend full of life one day might be killed the next," she went on. "Maybe that was so common that it gave people a sense of urgency about today—made them realize that it might be the last time they met someone?"

"The olden days, huh . . . ?"

Rikyū had served as Tea master to the ruler Hideyoshi himself. After incurring Hideyoshi's wrath, his followers were slaughtered and Rikyū was ultimately ordered to end his own life. It really had been an age when sharing a meal with someone was, all too often, a once-in-a-lifetime experience.

"Plus, there were no phones, and no planes or trains, so everyone traveled around on foot, didn't they?" Yukino warmed to her argument. "It wasn't as easy to meet up with people then as it is now. And they really can't have known whether they'd ever see each other again after saying farewell."

Living in the modern world, we never think, *This might be the last time we meet.*

We parted at the usual place with the customary "See you next week."

On the day of the spring equinox in March 1990, the weather was warm and sunny. Out of the blue, my father called me and said, "I had an errand in your neighborhood and I was thinking about dropping in to see you."

It was almost unheard-of for my father to phone me himself. However, an old classmate of mine had come to visit me that day. I told this to Dad, and he said, "Okay, never mind. That's fine. I'll see you some other time."

My friend and I talked until late that night. After she had gone home, I was somehow seized by the urge to see my father. For some curious reason, the fact that I had not seen him earlier when he had taken the trouble to call was playing on my mind.

It was already past eleven. If I went to my parents' house now, it would be too late to get a train back again. Normally, I would never have even considered going at this time of night. But it was gnawing at me. I wanted to see Dad. It was not that we had anything in particular to talk about. It would be enough just to see his face.

While I was hurriedly getting ready to go out, I phoned home to let them know that I was popping over.

"Is Dad there?" I asked.

"Hmmm? He's already gone to bed," said Mom, sounding unconcerned.

Somewhat reassured by this, I chatted with her for a while.

"You'll come and see us on your way home from Tea again, won't you?" she asked.

"Yeah, I'll drop in on Saturday," I replied.

And then I took off my coat again.

*

Later that week, on Friday evening, the phone on my desk rang. I picked up the receiver and heard Mom's voice. She sounded completely distraught. "Your father's collapsed! Come quickly!"

Three mornings later, my father took his final breath in the hospital without ever regaining consciousness.

Okay, never mind. That's fine. I'll see you some other time. These had turned out to be my father's last words to me.

At the hospital, my younger brother told me that Dad had been looking forward to seeing me. "Noriko's coming tomorrow, so let's have a family dinner," he had said on the morning of his collapse. "Rice with bamboo shoots would be nice."

I knocked my head repeatedly against the white wall as I tried to recall the last time we had all eaten together as a family.

When had it been?

I was frantically trying to wind back the clock. I wished I could return to the past. And I knew that I could not. Never again would the four of us be together as a family, something I had once seen as so trite and banal. *Never again*: those ice-cold words left me frozen with grief.

For everyone we know, there inevitably comes a day that marks a watershed, after which we never meet them again.

In his cups, my father would often turn to the rest of the family and say, "When I die, I want to go quickly, just like the cherry blossom."

He was always saying melodramatic things like that, so Mom, my brother and I would simply laugh and say, "Oh, he's off

145

again!" But on the day of Dad's funeral, the cherry blossom really did flutter from the trees, just like the finale of a play.

Sensei had been kind enough to accompany us to the crematorium. She whispered to me, "Oh, Noriko. The cherry blossom will hold such sad memories for you now."

Watching the gray smoke, I replied, "He really did go quickly . . ."

Life's events are always sudden, no matter when they come. In Rikyū's day, just as now . . .

There are some things you can't prepare yourself for even if you do have prior knowledge of them. In the end, you can't help but feel sad, caught off guard by unfamiliar emotions. Only then do you realize what you have lost.

But what other way is there to live? You can never prepare yourself before the worst happens, and after it does, all you can do is wait as you gradually get used to the grief.

This is why I firmly, firmly believe that if you want to get together with someone, you have to do so. If you love someone, you have to tell them so. When the flowers bloom, celebrate. When you fall in love, dive right in. When joy comes to you, share it with others. When you find happiness, embrace and savor it wholeheartedly. Perhaps that is all we can do.

If someone is special to you, you should seize every opportunity to eat with them, live life with them, and enjoy their company.

That, it turns out, is the meaning of *ichi-go ichi-e* . . .

CHAPTER 12

Listen for the Voice Within

The Cold Season

In 1990, a new student joined our Saturday lesson. Her name was Keiko Uozumi, and she was a single woman in her forties who worked for the government.

She told us she had never taken Tea lessons before. Most people are in their twenties when they start learning Tea, so a novice her age was unusual.

"Why did you decide to take up Tea?" one of us asked.

"I wanted to make time to relax and find myself again," she explained.

She started by learning how to fold her *fukusa* and walk across the tatami, like the rest of us. Rather than relaxed, she turned out to be painfully tense. When performing *o-temae*, she would grasp the *chashaku* so hard that her knuckles would whiten. Sensei often had to remind her to loosen her grip a little.

She was the most awkward first-year student of Tea that had ever joined our group. Given how tightly wound she was, we were all privately wondering how long she would last, and whether Tea might be too difficult unless you started learning while still young.

But Ms. Uozumi did not quit. Three years later, she was finally at ease with *o-temae*. She suddenly started to describe the things she noticed around her in vivid terms.

"Oh, the water in the washbasin outside sounds mellower! You can tell that spring is here."

and

"Rain's on the way—I can smell it in the air."

Sitting comfortably on a woven rush mat and stroking its green surface, she declared, "I do love the scent of new tatami!"

Despite setting out on the Way of Tea later than the rest of us, Ms. Uozumi had actually developed a keener enjoyment of the tea room than anyone. "I'm stuck in a concrete building during the week, day in, day out," she told us. "Tea gives me a golden opportunity to get in touch with the seasons once a week."

It took five years before I realized that Ms. Uozumi gradually became less talkative around November each year.

"I'm always like this once the nights start drawing in . . ." she said, quietly. She tended to withdraw into her shell, she told me, losing herself in reveries and spending the long, quiet evenings on the minutiae of daily life.

Come to mention it, I do that too . . .

Every year, once *furo* season began and the south-facing garden could be seen through the open tea room door, I would feel outgoing, brimming with energy and eager to start something new. Conversely, in *ro* season, when the tea room door was kept closed, my gaze instinctively turned inward. Huddling around the sunken hearth and watching the glowing charcoal, I would become more introspective.

"I do like this season too, though . . ." she said, seemingly pondering the idea. "I mean, it's great being active in the summer, but it's also nice to have a few months where you can hole up indoors. There's no need to choose which is good and which is bad: they're both good in their own ways."

This woman, who only started learning Tea after devoting half her life to her career, had again discovered a penetrating insight that had eluded those of us who had begun in our youth.

Listening to her words, I once more became keenly aware of the cycle of human emotion—the seasons of the mind. Just like the tea room switches from open to closed, our minds also change with the passing months. Opening, closing, opening again . . . Over and over, like breathing.

Society only values the bright and the positive. People forget that there can be no light without its opposite. You only get real depth when you have both. There is no need to choose one: they are equally good in their own ways. People need both.

When the Wind through the Pines Stops

At that first *chakai* I attended with my cousin Michiko, Sensei pointed out something on the outer wall of an old tea house in the manicured garden.

"That thing beside the entrance is a sword rack," she said. "Samurai would hang their weapons on it before crawling into the tea room."

In days gone by, knowledge of Tea was an essential accomplishment for any man of status, including high-ranking warriors. Toyotomi Hideyoshi even took Rikyū with him to the battlefield to make tea.

However, *chakai* today were a sea of women, their speech punctuated with mild exclamations of "My, my." It was hard to believe now that Tea had once been a male pursuit. To think that warriors who had raced across bloody battlefields and plotted against their rivals in deadly power struggles had been followers of the Way of Tea . . .

"It must have been like those secret backroom meetings that modern politicians have at exclusive old restaurants," Michiko said to me.

"Secret meetings?" I echoed. "Yes, I guess so."

Twenty years had passed since then. I was now forty.

Confucius said, "At forty I had no more doubts," but for me that was far from the truth. A whole host of problems threatened to overwhelm me. The worrying direction of my career. Troubles at home. My elderly mother. My own future . . .

In my twenties, as my desperation to find a job mounted, I had often fretted impatiently about wasting my Saturdays at Tea. But now I had hit my forties, I actually wanted to go to my lessons, especially when something was bothering me.

"When you sit in front of the kettle, you have to *be* in front of the kettle," Sensei would say. "You have to concentrate on emptying your mind."

But even after twenty years of Tea, I simply could not achieve that emptiness. My mind was always occupied with thoughts. Concerns about work. The need to tidy up after getting home.

Doubts, regrets, worries . . . They bubbled up endlessly, one after another.

It somehow felt to me that the older I grew, the further I was from achieving emptiness. I wanted to let my mind rest, but I could not. I would end up thinking even against my will. It was as though I had a little hamster in my head, constantly running in its wheel . . .

In the tea room, one sound can constantly be heard as a low, quiet undertone. We call it *matsukaze*: the wind through the pines. Small pieces of iron are attached with lacquer to the floor of the kettle specifically to generate this sound. When the water begins to boil, the "wind" comes and goes in waves: *shush-shush-shush-shush*.

Eventually, it becomes a single continuous *sssssssssshhhhhhhhh*.

Once the water reaches a rolling boil, it becomes a raging gale, whistling through the trees. *Matsukaze* and tea are inextricably intertwined.

One Saturday, Sanae was performing *o-temae* in her unhurried way. The only sound in the tea room as we gazed at her movements was the gentle susurration of that wind through the pines.

As usual, the hamster in my head was running in its little wheel, sending an endless stream of thoughts through my mind.

Ssssssssssssssshhhhhhhhhhhhhh

The whispering wind seemed to echo through my head as I listened to the constant chatter of my internal monologue.

The voice within and the sound without became one, blurring the boundaries between inside and out. The wind peaked as the water reached the boil, sending up a spiral of white steam. Sanae poured into the bubbling kettle a ladleful of cold water.

And the wind stopped dead.

.

.

.

My mind became a vacuum.

I thought of nothing. I worried about nothing. Those few seconds of tranquility had stilled my mind more completely than the deepest sleep. I held my breath and reveled in the moment. Perfect peace, like a short death.

Ahhhhhh . . .

Everyone in the room held their breath and surrendered themselves to the soothing silence. Time seemed to have stopped.

.

.

.

And then the wind again began to whisper through the pines.

Shush-shush-shush-shussshhh

The lull lasts no more than a few seconds. But I have never elsewhere experienced such a pleasurably profound pause.

It was then that I recalled Sensei telling us about the sword rack twenty years before.

Not only did samurai set their weapons down before entering the tea room, the entrances were intentionally designed to prevent them crawling through while carrying their long swords.

Freed from his onerous role in a cutthroat world, a samurai could return to being an ordinary person. I cannot begin to imagine the immense pressure experienced by the feudal warlords on whose shoulders rested the fate of a nation. Even the most intrepid warrior must have struggled to stave off the perpetual onslaught of worry, doubt, and dread.

That must be why those warlords sought emptiness so desperately.

A warrior's sword was second in importance only to his life, so maybe, when he left it outside that small doorway along with his status, he did so to seek a brief moment of deep peace in a society where emptying the mind was all but impossible. Perhaps he was pursuing the instant of profound serenity that came when he held his breath and relinquished himself to the void as the wind subsided . . .

Sssssssssssssshhhhhhhhhhhhhh

Softly, quietly, the wind whispers through the pines.

CHAPTER 13

When It's Raining, Listen to the Rain

Listen to the Rain

I will always remember that day.

It was a Saturday in June 1991, fourteen years after I began learning tea, and it had been raining since morning. The clinging humidity had made me listless. Going out on a wet day was already an unappealing idea, and then the downpour intensified after lunch.

Oh, I don't want to go to Tea . . .

We were all usually at Sensei's by one-thirty, but it was well past that. The rain continued without letup as the clock slowly ticked round to two-thirty. There was no sign that there might be a break in the deluge if I waited. When three o'clock approached, I finally got myself into gear and headed to Sensei's house through the pelting rain. It was hammering down so hard that I could barely see my way. By the time I burst into Sensei's entrance hall, my bright blue skirt had turned navy. A puddle immediately formed around my feet.

"Helloooo!"

Whether because the sound of the rain drowned out my voice or Sensei's customary "Come in!", I heard no reply. But in the middle of the step into the house proper lay a neatly folded pristine white towel. I could almost hear Sensei saying, "Use this to wipe your feet." I dried my soaking-wet feet and skirt as best I could, then changed into my white socks in the anteroom, as usual.

The house looked somehow different. The shutters over the sliding doors that faced south onto the garden were closed.

I padded along the dimly lit corridor and entered the tea room, apologizing for my tardiness. Ms. Uozumi was just whisking a bowl of *usucha*.

"You're late," said Sensei. "We were waiting for you. Hurry up and take your seat."

"Yes, Sensei."

I hastily sat down, forgetting to look at the *tokonoma*.

"Go on and eat your sweet," Sensei urged, placing a bright yellow Cochin ware sweet dish in front of me.

I briefly raised it in thanks with both hands and then opened the lid to reveal what looked like a small clump of hydrangeas.

"Wow!" I breathed.

Each one of the plump, round sweets was covered in tiny cubes of agar and perched on a real hydrangea leaf. Their colors varied like the flowers on which they were modeled: some were bluish, while others had a magenta or violet tinge.

My mouth curved upward in a spontaneous smile as I thought, *I'm glad I came after all!*

I picked up one of the bluer hydrangeas with the spicewood chopsticks and placed it on my *kaishi*. After taking another moment to appreciate its delightful form, I pressed my silver sweet pick against the agar. The jelly resisted slightly before the flower split in two, revealing the azuki paste inside. When I popped a piece into my mouth, the delectable sweetness of the bean paste mingled with the coolness of the agar.

The *chasen* went *swish-swish-swish-swish* . . .

A fresh, powerful aroma spread through the muggy room as the steaming bowl of caffeine-rich *matcha* was proffered. It was a vivid green, like rain-soaked moss.

"Thank you for the tea you have prepared."

After getting drenched on my walk to Sensei's house, the hot, slightly bitter tea was wonderfully invigorating. I could not keep myself from saying, 'Ah, that tastes so good!"

Despite my reluctance to leave my apartment, now that I was actually here, I felt somehow refreshed. The memory of being soaked to the skin on the way now seemed positively exhilarating.

I'd forgotten how much I like Tea on a rainy day!

Once the *o-temae* was over, the *hishaku* and *futaoki* were displayed atop the *tana*. The ceramic *futaoki* was dark green and shaped like a curled-up hydrangea leaf. On the leaf was a tiny blob, about the size of a pea—a cute little snail.

Oh, yes! Of course . . .

Every year, when I saw the snail on this *futaoki*, a childhood memory came back to me. During rainy season, I had stood under my yellow umbrella and watched a baby snail—just like this one—on top of a hydrangea leaf.

I remember now—just like every rainy season . . .

We have to forget so that we can remember again.

"Now, Yukino, I'd like you to replenish the charcoal," said Sensei.

After the *sumi-temae*, we examined the incense container. It was a round, flat, Kamakura-bori lacquerware box. I could not quite make out what it represented, but the prescribed dialogue gave me the chance to assuage my curiosity.

"What is the design of this incense container?" I asked.

"It is a sedge hat," replied Yukino, placing both hands on the tatami in the formal custom as she spoke.

"Oh!" I cried.

I had seen something like it in an old woodblock print of travelers on a wet day, wearing raincoats woven from straw and hats made of sedge. That was how they had kept dry in the olden days.

Spread out behind the brazier and its kettle was a short wooden folding screen with an openwork design of circles at its base. In some places, large and small circles overlapped.

"This is a brazier screen with water drop pattern," Sensei told us.

It represented ripples spreading across a puddle as the rain fell.

Hydrangeas, tiny snails, a sedge rainhat, ripples on a puddle . . . Everything I saw evoked Japan's rainy season in some way.

All at once, the deluge intensified. It felt as if Sensei's house was under a waterfall. In fact, it was rather frightening.

With the shutters on the southerly side closed but the rest open, the tea room was enveloped in a gloomy, peculiar atmosphere. I felt quite helpless in the face of that overwhelming noise. It reminded me of nights when a typhoon was raging outside. Despite my anxiety, it was oddly thrilling, and I suddenly felt a closer connection to everyone around me.

The rain pounded the roof and windows, all but drowning out every other sound within the wooden house. The downpour was so loud that I could visualize it as clearly as if I could actually see the scene outside.

Vapor spraying up from the black-tiled roof like white steam. Muddy water splattering as it surged out through the spouting. All the foliage in the garden left bedraggled by the cloudburst.

Fat raindrops bouncing off the broad leaves of the paperplant with a rattle like a fusillade of dried beans. Shining wet camellia leaves trembling slightly. The sodden, drooping blades of the broad-leaf bamboo. The young leaves of the grapevine under the eaves rustling as the deluge whipped them about, exposing their pale undersides. The whole garden wild with joy as the torrential rain washed over each and every leaf.

Water cascading onto the eaves from the roof with a *rat-tat-tat*. Giant puddles with surfaces churning so hard in the rain they looked like fish scales. Cars throwing up spray as they drove along the road, its asphalt surface transformed into a river.

I felt as if I could hear every single raindrop.

It was something like listening to music, when you can identify each instrument from its timbre: bass drum, timpani, marimba, maracas . . . And it was interwoven with similar clusters of sound from further away, forming a magnificent, multilayered symphony of rain.

Never before had I listened so intently to the rain. I felt as though I was plunging into a jungle of torrential noise. My heart pounded. It was raw and terrifying. But I wanted to keep going, even deeper. I was nothing but a pair of ears.

My hearing seemed to suddenly sharpen as I pushed past some kind of barrier.

Huh?!

For a moment, my ears felt as though they were blocked. All at once, I was in a huge open space where silence reigned.

.

.

.

Where was I?

Nothing stood in my way.

The strain of trying not to get the procedure wrong, my ever-present work worries, the chores waiting for me at home that day . . . It was all irrelevant.

The nagging worry that I needed to make more effort, the anxiety that I might be worthless without approval from others, the fear of my weaknesses being exposed . . . It all vanished.

I was incredibly free. I felt as if large, tepid raindrops were pelting down, stinging my skin. It was like I was squealing with childish delight as the downpour washed over me so powerfully that I could not open my eyes. I had never known such freedom before.

My horizons stretched out forever.

I had always been here. There was no need to go anywhere else.

Nothing was forbidden.

Nothing was compelled.

Nothing was lacking.

Just *being* was satisfaction in itself.

Another squall of driving rain dispelled the sensation. My ears seemed to unblock, and I was back in the room, sitting just where I had been.

The experience could only have been seconds long. Certainly less than a minute. Then, recalling that I had not yet looked at the *tokonoma* that day, I glanced behind me. I had to twist my body round and look up to see the short scroll. Written on it were two large characters:

Chō-u

. . . Oh! "Listen to the rain"!

I could not tear my eyes away.

Surrounded by the din of the lashing cloudburst, I felt as though I had been through a decisive moment. It was as if a locked door had opened in response to a magic word.

In fact, I had seen this scroll before. But I had thought that Sensei had chosen a scroll about rain because it was raining. I had merely regarded the characters as symbols to be decoded.

Now they seemed to speak to me.

"When it's raining, listen to the rain. You've got to be right *here*, in body *and* mind. Use all five senses and immerse yourself in savoring the now. If you do that, you'll understand. The path to freedom is always here, now."

We torment ourselves constantly with regrets about the past and worries about a future yet to come. But we can never go back to bygone days or prepare ourselves in anticipation of things to come, no matter how much we fret.

We cannot feel at ease in our lives as long as we are thinking about the past or the future. There is only one path: to savor the now. Only when we forget about past and future and just immerse ourselves in the moment do we realize that we are living in complete freedom, with nothing to stand in our way.

The rain fell relentlessly. I sat where I was, almost breathless with emotion.

When it's raining, listen to the rain. When it's snowing, look at the snow. Savor the heat in summer and the biting cold in winter. Relish each day to its fullest, whatever that day might bring.

This way of life is enshrined in Tea.

Living like this can help you appreciate the joy in everything you encounter, even situations that those around you would describe as terrible predicaments.

When it rains, we call the weather bad. But, really, there is no such thing as bad weather. If you can appreciate even the rain, every day becomes a good day.

Every day a good day?

The words rang a bell in my mind. I had encountered them somewhere before. Many, many times . . .

Something made me lift my gaze to the picture rail. There, in the dimness, I saw the framed piece of calligraphy where it always was.

Nichinichi kore kōjitsu

Oh!
Every day is a good day.
What a curious coincidence! I shivered.

Everything in here—including me—was connected, woven together like threads in a single bolt of fabric.

That piece of calligraphy had hung there since my very first visit to Sensei's house. The same characters had been written on the scroll at the first *chakai* she took us to. I had stared at the words many times since.

They had been right in front of me the whole time, but I had not really seen them until now.

Their message came through loud and clear, echoing in my heart: "Open your eyes. Our lives are a stream of perfect opportunities to discover that we can enjoy every day, no matter what it might bring. Exactly as you seem to have realized just now."

I felt as though I was standing straight and tall in the great outdoors, confronting the world as the rain poured down on me.

I took a deep breath and thought, with total clarity, *I have to remember how I feel right now, every day of my life!*

CHAPTER 14

Growth Takes Time

What Is Taught and What Is Not

In the autumn of my fifteenth year studying Tea, Yukino and I learned the *o-temae* called *bonten*. It was the final stage in my long journey, which had started with the basics of *usucha-*, *koicha-*, and *sumi-temae* before moving on to the assorted variations known as *naraigoto*—literally "things to learn"—and then up through the increasingly complex procedures of *satsūbako*, *karamono*, and *daitenmoku*.

But there is no such thing as graduation in Tea. I still spent my lessons practicing *o-temae* over and over, regular as clockwork, with the same prompts from Sensei as always: "Pick it up with your right hand and transfer it to your left," or "Place it on the second wale of the tatami," referring to the ridges formed by the weave of the rush mats.

Truth be told, I had been harboring doubts about something for the last ten years . . .

Sensei only ever talked about *o-temae*. That had been perfectly natural when I had just started learning, of course. But even after three, four, five years passed and I had made at least some progress, all she ever talked about was specific movements or sequences: "Make sure you scoop the hot water from the bottom of the kettle," or "Hold the *hishaku* a little higher when you pour."

Isn't there more to Tea than just o-temae?

When I began to notice changes in myself—appreciating seasons that I had never previously noticed, or finding my senses somehow altered—my qualms only intensified.

Why doesn't Sensei talk about anything other than o-temae? *Are the procedures really that important? If I can do* o-temae *perfectly, what then?*

But despite my misgivings, Sensei stayed focused on correcting my *o-temae* in painstaking detail as five years became ten and more.

"You know," she explained, "as time goes by and you get used to a procedure, little quirks creep in, or you start to miss out a subtle movement here and there. That's why it's important to perform *o-temae* properly every time, pouring your heart into every detail just like you did when you started to learn Tea."

I had the impression that Sensei was not interested in our personal insights. I was adamant that I would have talked about those insights if I had been a teacher.

But after starting to study *chaji* in my thirteenth year, the pieces of the jigsaw began to fall into place, giving me a clearer view of what Tea really was. So occasionally, during the silences when time itself seemed to stop, I would think, *Perhaps Sensei just doesn't talk about those things, even if she does feel them . . .*

Sensei would sit perfectly still, her eyes lightly closed as though listening to something. She seemed to be trembling slightly. When she opened her eyes, her expression suggested that she was about to speak. But then those eyes would simply crinkle into a smile as she gently breathed out.

It was during the downpour that Saturday in June, when I had looked at the scroll which read "Listen to the rain," that I first felt I might have an inkling of why she did not speak.

I, too, had been unable to put it into words . . .

Anything I could have said would have missed the essence of that experience by a mile. Feelings and emotions surpass the reach of words. That was why all I had been able to do was sit wordlessly, gulping down a torrent of emotion as big as I was. Trapped inside with no outlet, those feelings could only sting at my eyes.

.

.

.

That hushed moment had brought home to me with almost painful clarity how little we can see of what is inside the hearts of others.

Anyone looking into a tea room would see only people sitting in silence while someone prepares *matcha*. However, even at that moment, something else is happening, invisible to any observer.

This is the richest of silences.

.

.

.

It is a silence enshrouding a struggle between the burning desire to share the experience, the hollowness of knowing that words cannot adequately convey it, and the anguish of being left unable to speak.

I never knew that silence could be so intense . . .

*

It seemed to me that, side by side amid the stillness, Sensei and I shared the same feeling. Sensei might not have opened her mouth, but her silence spoke volumes about what words could not articulate.

What she was really teaching us lay beyond *o-temae*.

Whenever I opened the door and stepped into Sensei's entrance hall, the first thing I saw was always some flowers and a card inscribed with a piece of calligraphy, placed on top of the shoe cupboard. On hot days, the trickle of water into the stone washbasin became a stream. When I lifted the lid of a sweet dish, beautiful *wagashi* were lined up inside. In the *tokonoma* were flowers freshly picked that morning and a scroll. The *mizusashi, natsume*, tea bowl, *futaoki* . . .

Everything had a seasonal association and a link to the theme of the day. It was all part of Tea's spirit of hospitality. But Sensei never mentioned it. That was why I noticed only one or, at most, two things initially. After twenty years, I could spot three or even four. It was only once I started to identify these things for myself that I realized how much thought Sensei would put into demonstrating her hospitality toward us, preparing these seasonal touches without knowing when we would notice them. In fact, there were probably a whole host of little artifices arranged by her that were still going over our heads.

In her position, I would probably want to tell my students about what I was doing for them. But some things you just can't convey in words.

169

Sensei was waiting patiently for our minds to grow enough to discover all this for ourselves.

When I had just started learning, I constantly asked, "Why?" Sensei always replied, "It doesn't matter why. That's just the way it is in Tea."

This was astounding to me. I had been taught in school that if I did not understand something, I should ask questions until I did, and I resented Tea's apparently feudalistic tendencies.

But things I had not understood then were now becoming clear to me, one by one. Ten years pass, fifteen, and then one day you suddenly realize, "Oh! *That's* what that meant!" The answers came of their own accord.

Tea was all about physically experiencing the aesthetics and philosophy of the traditional Japanese way of life, which sets great store on living in harmony with the changing seasons.

It takes time to truly learn things. But after each lightbulb moment, that knowledge became part of my flesh and blood.

If Sensei had explained everything to us from the start, the long process would not have culminated in the reward of finding the answers for myself. She had left ample room in the margins for these encounters.

I had been convinced that if I was a teacher, I would tell my students all about the joy of these insights. But now I realized that this would deprive them of the pleasure of discovery, solely for my personal satisfaction.

*

Sensei taught us about procedure and nothing but procedure. But she was also trying to teach us through what she did *not* teach. In this way, she was setting us free.

For procedure is *all* there is. Yes, Tea procedure itself is strict, leaving little freedom. But apart from procedure, there are no other rules or limitations.

At school we learn how to find a predetermined "right answer" within a set time. The students who come up with the right answer fastest are hailed as the brightest, while poor grades await those who take too long, or give a different answer, or simply cannot fit into that system.

But there are no deadlines for discoveries in Tea. Each person is free to take as long as they need to understand, be it three years or twenty. When the time comes to notice something, you will notice it. Everyone matures at a different pace. The insight was just waiting for the right time for you.

Those who are faster on the uptake are certainly not regarded as better than others. The struggle to understand actually bred depth of character.

The answers were not a matter of right and wrong, or superior and inferior.

"The snow is white."

"The snow is black."

"It is not snowing."

These are all answers. Everyone is different, so their answers are, too. Tea accepts everyone just as they are.

Like in the board game Othello, black and white had been reversed in my mind. Once so convinced that Tea was a world that bound people with rules and forced them into a mold, I could now see that it offered complete freedom.

Our educational system prizes individuality, but pushing people to compete creates constraints and restrictions. In contrast, for all its formality and exacting rules, the world of Tea actually accommodates tremendous freedom by accepting individuals as they are.

What is true freedom?

What on earth are we competing for, anyway?

Both school and Tea aim to foster personal growth. But there is one major difference between them. At school, you are constantly comparing yourself to others. In Tea, you compare yourself with who you were yesterday.

I recalled a figure departing from a room: an elderly lady who must have been over eighty, with neatly coiffed pearl-white hair and a pale violet shawl wrapped lightly about her shoulders . . .

Michiko and I had met her at lunch that day at Sankeien, when Sensei had taken us to our first *chakai*. "Well, I'm off to study another session," the lady had said happily as she took her leave. "Studying is so much fun, isn't it?"

Fresh from cramming for university entrance exams, Michiko and I had thought the word "studying" incongruous on the lips of an octogenarian.

Years on, I have come to believe that there is another kind of studying, quite apart from our studies at school. It is not about giving the answers that you have been taught or competing over who is best. Rather, it involves grasping the answers for yourself, one insight at a time. It means using methods that suit you to build a path for growth that's right for you, just as you are.

You have to notice things. You have to attend to your growth as a person throughout your entire life.

In other words, studying means cultivating the self.

CHAPTER 15

Live in the Moment with an Eye to the Future

Zodiac Tea Bowls

Sensei often told Yukino and me, "You two ought to start teaching Tea somewhere. That's the best way to learn, you know."

We demurred: "Oh, we're not ready for that!"

In our fourteenth year of studying Tea, Yukino and I had both been awarded the plaque that proclaimed us qualified local instructors, but neither of us sought students of our own. We simply continued to attend our lessons as usual—for ten more years . . .

I had run up against a wall in my work many times. I had gone through low periods. There had been more partings and fresh encounters.

Radical changes transformed the world around me. Companies that had seemed rock-solid crumbled, while systems thought to be eternal and unchanging collapsed.

As for me, when Saturday came, I always went to Tea.

Amid the scent of the charcoal and the sound of the wind through the pines from the kettle, I would put thoughts of myself on hold as I opened up my heart completely to my five senses.

Bathed in the white light that filtered through the sliding paper screens, I would watch intently as someone swished a *chasen* back and forth, then eat *wagashi*, drink the hot tea, and slowly exhale.

I'm part of the seasons, too. All I need to do is connect to them like this.

This emotion would bubble up from the deepest recesses of my heart and my gaze would, for no reason, suddenly mist over with tears. And then I would return home invigorated, feeling quite different from when I had arrived.

I went to Tea to immerse myself in reality.

Six days into 2001, our annual *Hatsugama* at Sensei's house began at half-past eleven. With all the students assembled, the greetings got underway. "Happy New Year, everyone," Sensei said.

"Happy New Year!" we chorused in reply.

Dressed in a single-crested chocolate-brown kimono, her hands still lightly touching the tatami, Sensei added, "I'd like to thank all of you for accompanying me on this journey for so long, despite all my shortcomings. I'm truly grateful."

I wondered what had moved Sensei to say that to us on this particular occasion. I was surprised and touched.

Sensei had been forty-four years old when I had started learning Tea at the age of twenty. Twenty-four years later, I was the same age she had been then, which made her sixty-eight.

Her daughter had married and Sensei was already a grand-mother. The "Aunt Takeda" I had known then had been soft and plump as a *habutae-mochi* rice cake, but now she was small and thin, albeit as neatly turned-out as ever.

She always took care to cultivate her relationships with others, but was never clingy. Her demeanor and tone of voice never changed, no matter whose company she was in. She would express her thoughts plainly like a true native of Yokohama, crisp and to the point. Despite the passage of time, Sensei had not altered one jot.

"*Hatsugama* has come around again," she continued. "I know we repeat the same events year in, year out, but I've come to appreciate something recently: happiness is being able to do the same thing every year."

There certainly was a lot of repetition in Tea. The seasons came around like clockwork: spring, summer, autumn, winter, then back to spring, in an endless annual cycle. There was also another, even bigger cycle—a twelve-year period symbolized by the animals of the Japanese zodiac: mouse, ox, tiger, rabbit, dragon, snake, horse, sheep, monkey, chicken, dog, and wild boar.

A utensil evoking the new year's animal would make an appearance at every *Hatsugama*, without exception. In the year of the chicken, it was an incense container with a rooster motif. In the year of the tiger, it was a tea bowl decorated with an illustration of a papier-mâché tiger good luck charm. These would reappear in the same order every twelve years.

Each full rotation of the seasons took us another year forward in the twelve-year cycle of the zodiac, just like Earth spins on its axis as it orbits the sun.

2001 was the year of the snake. On the front of the *usucha* bowl was the ancient kanji that represented the snake in the zodiac.

Tea utensils associated with these twelve animals can only be used in the appropriate year. Even then, they cannot be used all year round—just the first and last lessons of the year.

We would always round off the year with the zodiac animal tea bowl and a scroll that read "*Mazu konnen buji medetaku senshūraku*—Rejoice in having safely reached the end of another year."

After that, the bowl would be put into its wooden box and tucked away somewhere at the back of the cupboard, whereupon it would not see the light of day until its turn came around again in another twelve years.

I found this out at my first *Hatsugama*.

"No!" I exclaimed. "Once every twelve years? But that means you can only use this bowl three or four times in your life!"

"That's right," replied Sensei.

"And you still went ahead and bought it, Sensei?" I asked, incredulous. She admitted that this was so. I could barely believe my ears. Tea had seemed inconceivably extravagant to me.

Looking now at that very same zodiac tea bowl, I remembered my initial astonishment and felt a rush of nostalgia for my twenty-year-old self. It was the third time I had held this bowl bearing the snake kanji . . .

I slurped the last mouthful of *usucha* and then examined the bowl, cradling it in both hands as I turned it.

I was thirty-two the last time I drank usucha *from this tea bowl. It was just after I'd managed to get my book published. Next time I drink from it, I'll be fifty-six. I wonder what kind of life I'll be living by then—who I'll be living it with, and where?*

"Last time we used this bowl, my son was still at university," said one of us, interrupting my reverie. "But now I've got two grandchildren at elementary school."

"I wonder what the world will be like the next time we see this tea bowl?" another mused.

"I hope we're still in good health," a third remarked.

"I'll be eighty by then!" Sensei told us.

We all burst out laughing.

When each of us gazed at the zodiac tea bowl, we were viewing our own lives from a great distance.

I wondered how many more times I would see this twelve-year cycle through.

Two more? Maybe three? And then I'll vanish from the face of the earth.

Tea rotates through the seasons as it revolves endlessly through the zodiac. But each of us will only experience that cycle six or seven times at most in our life.

This thought offers a glimpse of exactly how limited our time on this planet is. It made me want to cherish and savor that time precisely because it was so limited. I had the feeling that the zodiac tea bowl was telling me something: "Life has its ups and downs, but be patient; don't try to rush it. Take your time while you forge your character. Life means living in each and every moment, with an eye to the future."

I had gained a general sense of the rhythms of the Japanese seasons over the last twenty-four years. In the past I had complained about Sensei not letting us practice the same *o-temae* over and over until we had mastered it, but I had come to realize that Tea is all about enjoying those changes. I had memorized the names of many tea room flowers. I could cross a tatami mat in six steps without thinking. I appreciated the exquisite beauty of *wagashi* in all their glory. I even had a number of favorite phrases from hanging scrolls . . .

After all these discoveries, there would come moments when I realized in my own way what Tea was all about. But as soon as I heard teachers at a *chakai* discussing the elegant shape of a Raku tea bowl's mouth, or the beauty of a pattern of lines carefully imprinted in the ash of the *furo*, or the brush strokes of a scroll by a Zen master, it seemed like another world to me again.

Ultimately, what I thought of as Tea was no more than the minuscule fragment visible to me. The full picture remained almost entirely beyond my comprehension. Even now, I still know nothing . . .

But on the other hand, I also think that this is what Tea is—a polyhedron with an infinite number of faces.

Some people say that Tea is the formal aesthetics of a long-gone way of life. Some think of it as a compendium of Japanese arts. One writer even described it as a religion of beauty that pursues emptiness through single-minded devotion to the practice of *o-temae*. Others have called it an assemblage of wisdom for living in tune with the seasons, or even a style of Zen . . .

Tea permits any interpretation. Which means that my perspective is just one of myriad worlds of Tea.

Maybe Tea simply reflects the person, and there are as many forms of Tea as there are people.

"You really must try teaching," said Sensei. "It teaches you so many things itself, you know."

In our twenty-fifth year of Tea, Yukino and I took the first step toward obtaining the qualification of full Tea master.

Walking side by side on our usual way home, one of us said to the other, "I have a feeling our real lessons in Tea are about to begin."

"Yes, this is where it all starts . . ."

AFTERWORD

Afterword

These essays cover just a fraction of what I have experienced through Tea over the last twenty-five years. There was so much more I wanted to describe that my original manuscript was much longer, but I had to cut it down by half.

A lot of things I simply could not put into words. They unfolded before me endlessly, too far and too fast for me to keep up. How could I convey the spaces of the mind that lie hidden from physical view? I don't know how many times I found myself at my desk, staring dazedly into space.

First and foremost, by the standards of the Tea world, I am still just a child. For someone so green around the edges to write an entire book about Tea seemed foolhardy in the extreme. But Tea accepts us in all our imperfection and I wrote this book as a way of plunging headlong into that all-encompassing embrace. Please do tell me of any mistakes—I will welcome feedback most gratefully.

In Japanese, some prefer to read the kanji for "Every day is a good day" with the pronunciation *Nichinichi kore kōnichi*. But both *kōnichi* and *kōjitsu* are widely used, and we read it *kōjitsu* at Sensei's, so I opted for the reading familiar to me. I have also disguised everyone's identities with pseudonyms.

No words can fully express my gratitude to Sensei, who, for twenty-five years, taught me to enjoy the heat of summer and the cold of winter and showed me the boundless horizons of freedom that lie beyond the rules dictating every movement of hand and foot. I dedicate this book to her. Sensei, this is what Tea means to me now.

To everyone who attended Tea lessons with me, to my friends who provided practical help and emotional support throughout the long process of writing this book, to my mother and cousin who encouraged me to take up Tea in the first place, I say thank you.

Last, but not least, I want to thank Noriko Shimaguchi of Asuka Shinsha for her assistance over many years. Without her passion and tenacity for making books, I would not have been able to complete this book. I would like to take this opportunity to express my heartfelt gratitude to her.

In my twenty-sixth year of studying Tea . . .

Noriko Morishita
Early Spring, 2002

TEA TERMS

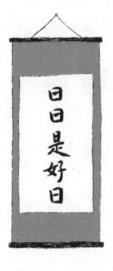

A Selected List of Tea Terms

* Denotes terms that do not appear in the text, but which are included here for reference.

chabana	*flowers for the tea room*
chaire	*tea container*

chaire

chaji	*a formal tea gathering, including a meal, for a small number of invited guests*
chajin	*Tea practitioner*
chakai	*tea gathering*
chasen	*bamboo tea whisk*

chasen

chasen set in a tea bowl

*chashitsu	*tea room*
*chatsubo	*earthenware tea jar*
*chawan	*tea bowl*

chawan

chiriuchi	*snapping the fukusa to symbolically cast off any dust*
daisu	*large, black-lacquered formal utensil stand*

dashibukusa	*silk cloth used by guests when drinking thick tea*

 dashibukusa

fukusa	*silk cloth used to cleanse the tea container and tea scoop when preparing tea*

 *fukusa*

furo	*brazier*

 furo

futaoki	*lid rest*
haiken	*examining the tea utensils*
*hanaire	*vase*
hishaku	*bamboo ladle*

 hishaku

jikyaku	*second guest*

kaiseki	*the multi-dish meal served as part of a chaji*
kaishi	*the paper on which sweets are placed*
***kakejiku**	*hanging scroll*
karamono	*tea utensils from China (literally, "Tang things")*
kensui	*waste water bowl*

kensui

***kōgō**	*incense container*
koicha	*thick tea*
***kuromoji**	*spicewood chopsticks*
***kyaku**	*guest*

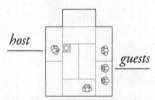

host — *guests*

maki-e	*a technique for decorating lacquerware with silver and gold powder*
matcha	*powdered green tea*
matsukaze	*"wind through the pines": the sound made by the water boiling in the kettle*
mizusashi	*water jar*
mizuya	*a kitchen-like room beside the tea room, where the host makes their preparations*

natsume	*jujube-shaped lacquerware tea container*

 natsume

nerikiri	*dough made from white bean paste and glutinous rice flour*
***nijiriguchi**	*small, low doorway through which guests enter the tea room*

 nijiriguchi

***o-kama**	*kettle*
***o-keiko**	*Tea lesson*
o-temae	*Tea procedure*
***ocha wo tateru**	*whisk tea*
ro	*sunken hearth*

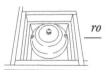 *ro*

***sahō**	*Tea etiquette*
***sankyaku**	*third guest*
***sensu**	*fan*
shōkyaku	*main guest*
sometsuke	*blue and white pottery*

*sukiyabukuro *pouch used to carry belongings necessary for Tea*

 sukiyabukuro

tana *portable shelf unit for displaying utensils*
*teishu *host*
tokonoma *alcove*

 *tokonoma*

*tsukubai *stone washbasin made from a hollowed-out rock*
usucha *thin tea*
*yōji *sweet pick*
yoritsuki *anteroom*

ABOUT THE AUTHOR

Photo by Sakurako Kuroda

Noriko Morishita was born in Yokohama, Kanagawa Prefecture in 1956. She graduated from the Department of Japanese Literature at the Faculty of Humanities, Japan Women's University. While still an undergraduate, she began working as a reporter, gathering stories for *Shūkan Asahi* magazine's popular column, *Dekigotology*. Since publishing her experiences as a writer in *Nori-yakko Dosue* (1987), she has enjoyed a flourishing career as an essayist and writer of reportage. Morishita's books include *Itoshii Tabemono* [My Darling Food] and *Kōjitsu Nikki—Kisetsu no yō ni Ikiru* [Good Day Diaries—Living in tune with the seasons], the sequel to *Nichi Nichi Kore Kōjitsu* [published in English as *The Wisdom of Tea*]. A film adaptation of *Nichi Nichi Kore Kōjitsu* (titled "Every Day a Good Day" in English) was released in 2018.

ABOUT THE TRANSLATOR

Eleanor Goldsmith was born in Swansea, Wales in 1976. She graduated from the Department of East Asian Studies at the University of Durham. She began studying the Urasenke tradition of the Way of Tea while working as a JET Program Coordinator of International Relations at Joetsu City Office, Niigata Prefecture. She has been a translator since 2000 and now lives in Auckland, New Zealand, where she continues to practice Tea. She is President of the Chado Urasenke Tankokai New Zealand Association.